Creative and Practical Projects

Kids' Party Cakes

Publisher's Note: Raw or semi-cooked eggs should not be consumed by babies, toddlers, pregnant or breastfeeding women, the elderly or those suffering from a chronic illness. When using water to stick sugarcraft items, it is safest to use cold boiled water, which is sterile.

Publisher & Creative Director: Nick Wells
Senior Project Editor: Catherine Taylor
Recipe text by: Ann Nicol, Wendy Sweetser and Jill Tipping
Picture Research: Esme Chapman
Art Director: Mike Spender
Layout Design: Jane Ashley
Digital Design & Production: Chris Herbert

Special thanks to Frances Bodiam.

For all cake decorating supplies, colours and shimmers by mail order: **Squires Kitchen**, Squires Group, Squires House, 3 Waverley Lane, Farnham, Surrey, GU9 8BB. Tel: 0845 617 1801 www.squires-shop.com

Discover 1000s more inspiring baking and decorating ideas, at **lakeland.co.uk.** For cookie cutters, sugarcraft supplies and bakeware by mail order: **Lakeland**, Alexandria Buildings, Windermere, Cumbria, LA23 1BQ. Tel: 01539 488 100.

For wheat-free and gluten-free flours and xanthan gum, **Doves Farm Food** sell through supermarkets and health food shops or contact them at www.dovesfarm.co.uk

This is a FLAME TREE Book

Flame Tree Publishing
Crabtree Hall, Crabtree Lane
Fulham, London SW6 6TY
United Kingdom
www.flametreepublishing.com

First published 2014

Copyright © 2014 Flame Tree Publishing Ltd

14 16 18 17 15
1 3 5 4 2

ISBN: 978-1-78361-225-3

A copy of the CIP data for this book is available from the British Library.

Printed in Singapore

Image credits: ©iStock.com and the following: GrenouilleFilms 4 & 224; jenfelix 9tr & 160tr & 178; ivanmateev 36tr & 152; RBOZUK 37tr & 232; luba 51 & 96; anopdesignstock 70br & 72; erierika 82; dnaveh 88; Yamac Beyter 160bl & 174; servet yigit 176; castillodominici 182; dendong 184; RicardoToledo 197bl & 240; clubfoto 204; Jodi Jacobson 216; fotonehru 230; BigKnell 234. Courtesy **Shutterstock.com** and the following: Krezodent 7 & 196bl & 220; Andrea Slatter 8bl & 161bl & 188, 69t & 71tl & 80, 144; John Kroetch 8br & 142, 84, 92, 98, 114, 119tl & 132, 146, 197tr & 212, 214; Ruth Black 8tr & 198, 45 & 94, 65 & 70bl & 78, 71bl & 86, 160br & 170, 161tr & 180; Rose-Marie Henriksson 9bl & 162; Ryan Carter 9tl & 118br & 136; bitt24 10; Sergio Bertino 11; tommaso lizzul 11b; Sea Wave 12; Gayvoronskaya_Yana 13; Hirurg 14; Dream79 15; 6493866629 16; Africa Studio 17t, 21b, 38; Joerg Beuge 17b, 23 t; Neftali 17c; endeavor 18c; Evikka 18b; gwolters 18t, 23 b; Crepesoles 19t, 22; Robyn Mackenzie 19c; Sychugina 19b; bonchan 20; sutsaiy 21t; Heath Johnson 24; JFunk 25b, 43 & 76; Robert Wolkaniec 25t; fholas 29; Patty Orly 34; Olga Lyubkina 35; Prezoom.nl 36br & 134, 110, 164, 197tl & 238; Vyaseleva Elena 36bl & 120; Andrey Starostin 37bl & 70tr & 232; Jiri Hera 39b; Scott Bolster 39t; CandyBox Images 41; Yalcin Sonat 47 & 140; Milleflore Images 49 & 196bl & 218, 210; humbak 54t; NataLT 54b; bernashafo 55t; Ryabitskaya Elena 56t; zstock 59 & 71tr & 100; fototip 60, 61, 62; artfood 67 & 130, 119tr & 126; flashgun 67t; CapPui 68t; Martin Nemec 69b & 156; Alekuwka 74; andras_csontos 106 & 188bl; Roberto Piras 108; Hannamariah 116; Denis Tabler 118tr & 158; Matthew Bechelli 119br & 154; urbanlight 122, 150; lanych 124; Petr Jilek 148; Dave Clark Digital Photo 161tl & 166; Gordana Sermek 168; Vezzani Photography 186; Pavlo Burdyak 190; Amero 192; Stakhov Yuriy 194; Audrey Yurlov 196tr & 208; Vahan Abrahamyan 200; Christina Richards 202; Brittny 206; nito 222; Margoe Edwards 226; Eponaleah 228. © **Foundry Arts:** 33, 37tl, 53, 55b, 58, 63, 64, 65t, 90, 104, 112, 128, 138. Courtesy of **LAKELAND:** 56b, 57b. Courtesy of **Getty Images** and: DK: Trish Gant 172; spencer Jones 236.

Creative and Practical Projects

Kids' Party Cakes

**FLAME TREE
PUBLISHING**

Contents

Introduction

A cake is the most important part of any child's celebration and making your own cakes is such fun and so much more satisfying than buying one from a shop. This book gives you all the help you will need to make a kid's cake, with lots of new ideas to help make yours look really special.

Even if you are just starting out as a baker, you will find the recipes easy to follow. Each project is illustrated with a beautiful photograph to inspire you and full instructions are provided to help you through all the decorating. The front section of the book tells you everything you will need to know about basic recipes and equipment, how to master covering techniques, piping and making decorations for a professional finish. If you don't have special cutters, you will find templates and stencils included at the back of the book to help you, along with guides on how to cut the cakes into special shapes. Icing and making decorations takes time and patience and it is important to read through the instructions carefully and allow yourself plenty of time to complete all the stages of the chosen cake. If a cake looks a little difficult you can bake and freeze it already cut into pieces for up to 4 weeks ahead to help reduce the last-minute work involved.

This book tries to cover as many themes to interest children as possible. Some of the cakes are aimed at the very young, while others are aimed at older children. In the Seasonal & Celebration section you will find bright and colourful cakes for special ages. Fantasy & Adventure includes cakes with imaginative themes including pirates, dragons and a castle for a princess. There is a section that features favourite animals – bears, butterflies and even pigs in a muddy pool, which will bring delight to small faces. Hobbies & Interests are always a favourite subject for party cakes and boys will be delighted with football, cricket and rugby cakes, while girls will love a 'Teddies in Tutus' cake, fashion-themed cakes or a 'Disco Diva' cake.

These cakes show a variety of styles, but you can have fun adapting them yourself and creating your own unique designs. Whatever your level of skill, I'm sure you will find a cake in this book to delight your child.

Ann Nicol

Cake
Basics

From the way they look to blowing out the candles, kids love everything about party cakes! To make sure they are not disappointed by the taste, brush up on your cake-baking basics by reading this chapter. Covering ingredients, equipment, basic cake-making techniques and basic cake recipes to refer to later, you will soon be up to speed and baking expert cupcakes and sponges ready to customize with that creative touch.

Ingredients

In baking, most cakes are made by mixing sugar, fats, flour and eggs together. During the mixing, air is incorporated into the mixture to greater or lesser degrees to make it rise during baking. As a cake mixture bakes, the strands of gluten in the flour are stretched and the heat hardens them to give a light, sponge-like texture.

Sugar

Sugar is not just included to give sweetness to cakes, it also produces a structure and texture that make a cake tender, so always choose the correct type for your recipe.

- Granulated Sugar – This is the standard sugar that you add to your tea. It comes in white and golden unrefined varieties and is used for toppings. The coarseness of granulated sugar means that it does not dissolve easily and is not designed for most baking recipes, so is no good for the creaming method.

- Caster Sugar – This is a fine-ground granulated sugar, which also comes in white and golden (or 'natural') unrefined varieties. It blends easily with butter and margarine when beaten or 'creamed' into light sponge mixtures.

- Soft Light and Dark Brown Sugars – These cream well and are usually used in richer cakes or spicy fruit mixtures such as carrot cake, and in recipes where rich colour and flavour are needed. Store this sugar in a tightly sealed container to prevent it from drying out. If it does become dry or lumpy, pound it back into crystals with the flat end of a rolling pin before you use it.

- ✎ **Muscovado Sugar** – This sugar is natural and unrefined, with a deep brown colour and rich flavour that makes fruit cakes extra special. It comes in light and dark varieties.

Eggs

- ✎ **Storing** – Always store eggs in the refrigerator, but remove them an hour or so before you start to bake, as better results will be achieved if you allow them to reach room temperature before using. This is because, at this temperature, eggs will whisk better and achieve more aeration.

  This not only gives more volume to the mixture, but also allows the eggs to blend in more easily. Cold eggs used straight from the refrigerator can curdle or split a mixture.

- ✎ **Egg Types** – Eggs sold as 'value' or 'economy' can be used for baking cakes and cupcakes, particularly if you are working to a budget (but do not forget the welfare issues involved in this choice). Also, do remember that these may be ungraded and of different sizes, so, for best results, buy eggs marked as 'medium' and 'large'. If you do use economy eggs, make sure to note the sizes you are using and try to even out the quantity by, say, using one large and two small eggs instead of three medium-size ones.

- ✎ **Egg Powder** – Dried egg-white powder gives good results and can be substituted in royal icing recipes, or in recipes where you are unsure about using raw egg whites in the case of pregnant women, the very young or the elderly.

✎ Ingredients

Flours

Plain white flour provides the structure of a cake, but contains nothing to make it rise, so cakes that do not need raising agents are made with plain flour. Most recipes using plain flour have bicarbonate of soda or baking powder added to them to make the cakes rise. It is always advisable to sift this into the mixture to incorporate the raising agents evenly.

∾ Self-raising Flour – This has raising agents already added, that will add air to make a cake rise, so is used for light sponge mixtures. If you have only plain flour available, add 2¹/₂ tsp baking powder to 225 g/8 oz plain flour to make it into a self-raising flour.

∾ Storing Flour – White flours should be stored in a cool, dry place for up to 6 months, but wholemeal flours will not keep as long, as they have a higher fat content, so check the use-by date on all packs. Flour is best stored in a sealed airtight container. Always wash and dry this thoroughly before refilling and never add new flour to old. Small micro-organisms will form in very old flour, from the protein, and these can be seen as tiny black specks that will spread into new flour. If you do not have a container, store the opened paper bag inside a large plastic bag and make sure all flour is kept dry. Damp flour weighs more and therefore alters the recipe, which could lead to heavy or flat cakes.

Raising Agents

Raising agents are added to flour to make cakes rise and produce a light texture. It is important to be accurate when measuring these fine powders out, so always use a measuring spoon.

- ∾ **Baking Powder** – This is a mixture of bicarbonate of soda and cream of tartar. When liquid is added, the powder fizzes and bubbles and produces carbon dioxide, which expands with heat during baking and gives an airy texture. Be careful not to use very hot or boiling liquid in mixtures, as these can reduce the power of baking powder.

- ∾ **Bicarbonate of Soda or Baking Soda** – This is a gentler raising agent and is often used to give melted or spicy mixtures a lift. Cakes will have a bitter flavour if too much is added, so measure this out carefully and accurately with a proper measuring spoon, not a domestic teaspoon.

Fats

Fat adds structure, texture and flavour to cakes and improves their keeping qualities. Always remove them from the refrigerator before using them – they are much easier to mix in when at room temperature.

- ∾ **Butter and Hard Block Margarine** – Butter and hard margarine can be interchanged in a recipe, and the results will be the same. Butter, however, will always give a better flavour to cakes, so, if they are for a special occasion, is it well worth spending a little extra on this.

- ∾ **Soft Margarine** – Sold in tubs, this is wonderful for using in all-in-one sponge recipes where all the ingredients are quickly mixed together in one bowl. This fat always produces good results and is quick and easy to use because it does not have to be used at room temperature but can be taken straight from the refrigerator. Do not substitute soft margarine for butter or hard block margarine in a recipe, as it is a totally different kind of fat, which will not produce the same results. Cakes using soft margarine usually require extra raising agent, so do follow the recipe carefully and do not be tempted to overbeat the mixture, as it will become wet and the cakes may sink. Up to 2 minutes of whisking with an electric mixer is fine to make a smooth mixture.

Ingredients

Spices

Most dried spices have a reasonably long shelf life, but will not keep indefinitely, and remember that they will gradually lose their aroma and flavour. It is a good idea to buy in small quantities only when you need them. You will find that both light and heat affect the power and flavour of spices, so, if stored in clear glass jars, keep them out of the light – the best place to store spices is in a dark, cool, dry place.

Flavourings

Flavouring extracts are very concentrated and usually sold in liquid form in small bottles. For example, a teaspoon measure will usually be enough to flavour a cake mixture for 12 cupcakes.

Vanilla and almond extracts are ideal to impart their delicate flavours into cake mixtures and you will find the more expensive extracts give a finer and more natural flavour. Rosewater can be used for flavouring both cake mixtures and icings and has a delicate, perfumed flavour. Fruit flavourings, such as lemon, lime, orange and raspberry, will give a fresh twist to mixtures and icings.

Chocolate

Indulgent chocolate is a useful ingredient for any cake decorator, whether used just to make the cake itself or as a delicious icing too. For the best results and a professional finish and flavour, it is always advisable to buy the highest-quality chocolate you can find, although this will be more expensive. Better-quality chocolates contain a higher percentage of real cocoa fat, which gives a flavour and texture far superior to cheaper varieties.

Cheaper chocolate labelled as 'cooking' or 'baking' chocolate contains a much lower percentage of cocoa solids and is best avoided in favour of better-quality eating chocolate.

The amount of cocoa fat or solids contained in chocolate will be marked on the wrapper of any good-quality chocolate. Those marked as 70 per cent (or more) cocoa solids will give the best results and you will find that this chocolate is shiny and brittle and it should snap very easily.

- **Dark Chocolate** – Also known as 'plain' or 'plain dark' chocolate, this is the most useful all-purpose type of chocolate for baking, as it has a good strong flavour.

- **Milk Chocolate** – Milk chocolate has sugar added and is sweeter than dark, so is also good for melting for icings and decorations.

- **White Chocolate** – This is not strictly chocolate, as it contains only cocoa butter, milk and sugar. It is expensive and the most difficult to work with, so must be used with care. It is best to grate it finely and keep the temperature very low when melting it.

- **Chocolate Cake Covering** – This is a cheaper substitute, which contains a minimum of 2.5 per cent cocoa solids and vegetable oil. It is considerably cheaper than real chocolate and the flavour is not as good, but it is easy to melt and sets quickly and well for a coating.

- **Cocoa Powder** – Cocoa powder needs to be cooked to release the full flavour, so blend it with boiling water to make into a paste, then cool, before adding to a recipe, or sift it into the bowl with the flour.

- **Drinking Chocolate** – Be aware that this is not the same as cocoa, as it contains milk powder and sugar. Some recipes may specify using drinking chocolate and these are successful, but do not substitute it for cocoa powder, as it will spoil the flavour of a cake.

　Ingredients

Key Equipment

Bakeware

It is worth investing in a selection of high-quality tins, which, if looked after properly, should last for many years. Choose heavy-duty metalware that will not buckle, or the new flexible silicone moulds – these are easy to turn out, most need very little greasing and they also wash and dry easily.

❧ **Deep Cake Tins** – With deep cake tins, you can buy both round or square tins, depending on preference. They vary in size from 12.5–35.5 cm/5–14 inches with a depth of between 12.5–15 cm/5–6 inches. A deep cake tin, for everyday fruit or Madeira cake, is a must, a useful size is 20 cm/8 inches.

❧ **Metal Muffin Trays** – Muffin trays come in different weights and sizes; they are generally available with six or 12 deep-set holes. When purchasing, buy the heaviest type you can – although these will be expensive, they produce the best results, as they have good heat distribution and do not buckle. Muffin trays can vary in the size and depth of hole, which obviously affects the eventual size of the muffin.

If using trays without a nonstick finish, it is advisable to give these a light greasing before use. To grease trays, apply a thin film of melted vegetable margarine with a pastry brush or rub round the tin with kitchen paper and a little softened butter or margarine. You will normally need to line metal muffin trays with deep paper muffin cases or strips of baking parchment.

- **Silicone Muffin Trays and Cupcake Cases** – These are flexible and produce very good results. Although they are sold as nonstick, it is still advisable to rub round each hole or case with a little oil on kitchen paper to prevent sticking. Silicone cupcake cases come in many bright colours and, unlike paper cases, are reusable. Simply wash out any crumbs after use in soapy water and leave them to dry, or clean them in the dishwasher.

- **Paper Cases** – These come in many varieties, colours and shapes. It is advisable to buy the more expensive types, which are thicker and give a good shape to the cake as it rises. Oil and moisture are less likely to penetrate through the thicker cases, whereas it may show through the cheaper ones. Metallic gold, silver and coloured cupcake cases give good results and create a stunning effect for a special occasion. Cupcake cases also come in mini-muffin sizes. These may not be so easy to find, but can be bought from mail-order cake decoration suppliers.

- **Cake Pop Baking Moulds** – These are metal tins that come in two halves and have 12 small, round indentations for the cake mix. Fill one half of the tin and clamp the other tin on top and, as the mixture rises, it will form perfect round shapes. The round cakes are placed on thin lollipop sticks before decorating.

- **Mini Cake Tins and Moulds** – These are small square or round domed cake tins that measure approximately 5 cm/2 inches across and make small individual cakes. You can buy mini cake pans using detachable grids that will make both square and round shapes.

- **Baking Papers and Foil** – Nonstick baking 'parchment' or 'paper' is useful for lining the bases of small tins or for drying out chocolate and sugarpaste shapes.

Key Equipment

Greaseproof paper is needed for making triangular paper icing bags. Baking parchment can be used, but greaseproof paper is better, as it is thinner and more flexible.

A large sheet of kitchen foil is handy for wrapping cakes or for protecting wrapped cakes in the freezer.

Useful Items

- **Mixing Bowls** – Three to four different sizes of mixing bowls are very useful for mixing and melting ingredients.

- **Wire Cooling Racks** – Another vital piece of equipment is a wire cooling rack. It is essential when baking to allow cakes to cool after being removed from their tins.

A wire rack also protects your kitchen surfaces from the heat and allows air to circulate around the goodies, speeding cooling and preventing soggy bottoms.

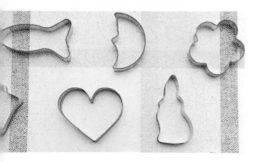

- **Measuring Items** – Baking needs 100 per cent accuracy to ensure a perfect result. Scales come in many shapes and sizes, both digital and with weights. Most have a weigh pan, although, with some, your own bowl is used. Measuring jugs and spoons are essential for accurate measuring of both your dry and wet ingredients.

- Mixing Spoons and Sieves – Basic mixing cutlery is also essential, such as a wooden spoon (for mixing and creaming), a spatula (for transferring the mixture from the mixing bowl to the baking tins and spreading the mixture once it is in the tins) and a palette knife (to ease cakes out of their tins before placing them on the wire racks to cool). Also, do not forget a fine-mesh sieve, for sifting flour and powders.

- Cake Tester or Skewer – Use a small, thin metal skewer for inserting into the centre of a cake to test if the cake is ready. This is a handy piece of equipment, but, if you do not have one, a clean, thin metal knitting needle may be used instead.

- Pastry Brush – A pastry brush is used for brushing glazes over cakes and melted butter round tins. As brushes tend to wear out regularly and shed their bristles, keep a spare new brush to hand.

- Palette Knives – A small and a large palette knife are ideal for many jobs, including loosening cakes from their tins, lifting cakes and swirling on buttercream icing. A palette knife with a cranked blade is useful for lifting small cakes or flat pieces of sugarpaste.

- Kitchen Scissors – Scissors are essential for many small jobs, including cutting papers to size and snipping cherries, dried fruits or nuts into chunks.

- Grater – A grater is useful for grating citrus zests, chocolate and marzipan/almond paste. Choose one with a fine and a coarse side.

Key Equipment

Electrical Equipment

Nowadays help from time-saving gadgets and electrical equipment makes baking far easier and quicker. There is a wide choice of machines available, from the most basic to the highly sophisticated.

Food Processors – When choosing a machine, first decide what you need your processor to do. If you are a novice, it may be a waste to start with a machine which offers a wide range of implements and functions.

This can be off-putting and result in not using the machine to its ultimate potential. When buying a food processor, look for measurements on the sides of the processor bowl and machines with a removable feed tube, which allows food or liquid to be added while the motor is still running.

Look out for machines that have the facility to increase the capacity of the bowl and have a pulse button for controlled chopping.

For many, storage is an issue, so reversible discs and flex storage, or, on more advanced models, a blade storage compartment or box, can be advantageous.

It is also worth thinking about machines which offer optional extras which can be bought as your cooking requirements change. Mini chopping bowls are available for those wanting to chop small quantities of food. If time is an issue, dishwasher-friendly attachments may be vital. Citrus presses, liquidisers and whisks may all be useful attachments for the individual cook.

∾ Table-top Mixers – Table-top mixers are freestanding and are capable of dealing with fairly large quantities of mixture. They are robust machines and good for heavy cake mixing as well as whipping cream, whisking egg whites or making one-stage cakes.

These mixers also offer a wide range of attachments ranging from liquidisers to mincers, juicers, can openers and many more and varied attachments.

∾ Hand-held Mixers – A hand-held electric mixer makes quick work of whisking butter and sugar and is an invaluable aid for cake baking. They are smaller than freestanding mixers and often come with their own bowl and stand from which they can be lifted and used as hand-held devices. They have a motorised head with detachable twin whisks.

These mixers are versatile, as they do not need a specific bowl in which to whisk. Any suitable mixing bowl can be used. Do not be tempted to use a food processor for mixing small amounts, as it is easy to over-process and this may produce flat cakes.

Key Equipment

Basic Cake-making Techniques

Lining Cake Tins

If a recipe states that the tin needs lining, do not be tempted to ignore this. Rich fruit cakes and other cakes that take a long time to cook benefit from the tin being lined so that the edges and base do not burn or dry out. Greaseproof paper or baking parchment is ideal for this. It is a good idea to have the paper at least double thickness, or preferably three or four thicknesses. Sponge cakes and other cakes that are cooked in 30 minutes or less are also better if the bases are lined, as it is far easier to remove them from the tin.

The best way to line a round or square tin is to lightly draw around the base and then cut just inside the markings, making it easy to sit in the tin. Next, lightly grease the paper so that it will easily peel away from the cake.

If the sides of the tin also need to be lined, then cut a strip of paper long enough for the tin. This can be measured by wrapping a piece of string around the rim of the tin. Once again, lightly grease the paper, push against the tin and oil once more, as this will hold the paper to the sides of the tin.

Separating Eggs

When separating eggs (that is, separating the white from the yolk), crack an egg in half lightly and cleanly over a bowl, being careful not to break the yolk and keeping it in the shell. Then tip the yolk backwards and forwards between the two shell halves, allowing as much of the white as possible to spill out into the bowl. Keep or discard the yolk and/or the white as needed. Make sure that you do not get any yolk in your whites, as this will prevent successful whisking of the whites. It takes practice!

Making Methods

- **Creaming** – Light cakes are made by the creaming method, which means that the butter and sugar are first beaten or 'creamed' together. A little care is needed for this method. Using a large mixing bowl, beat the fat and sugar together until pale and fluffy. The eggs are gradually beaten in to form a slackened batter and the flour is folded in last, to stiffen up the mixture. In some recipes, egg whites are whisked and added to the mixture separately for extra lightness.

  When the eggs are added, they are best used at room temperature to prevent the mixture from splitting or 'curdling'. Adding a teaspoon of flour with each beaten egg will help to keep the mixture light and smooth and prevent the mixture from separating. A badly mixed, curdled batter will hold less air and be heavy or can cause a sunken cake.

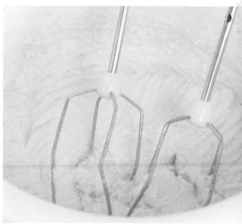

- **All-in-one Mixtures** – This 'one-stage' method is quick and easy and is perfect for those new to baking, as it does not involve any complicated techniques. It is ideal for making light sponges, but soft tub-type margarine or softened butter at room temperature must be used. There is no need for any creaming or rubbing in, as all the ingredients are simply placed in a large bowl and quickly beaten together for just a few minutes until smooth. Be careful not to overbeat, as this will make the mixture too wet. Self-raising flour with the addition of a little extra baking powder is vital for a good rise.

∾ Fruit Cakes – Rich fruit cakes are usually made by the creaming method, then dried fruits and nuts are folded into the mixture last.

Checking to See if the Cakes are Cooked

For light sponge-type cakes, press the centre lightly with the fingertips and, if the cake is cooked, it should spring back easily. To test more thoroughly, insert a thin, warmed skewer into the deepest part of the centre.

If the cake is cooked, it will come out perfectly clean with no mixture sticking to it, but, if there is some mixture on the skewer, bake the cake for a little longer and test again.

Small cupcakes should be golden, risen and firm to the touch when pressed lightly in the centre. The last part of a cupcake to cook is the centre, so, after the baking time stated, check this area.

How to Patch Up Mistakes

If the cakes are overcooked or are burnt on the outside, simply scrape this away with a serrated knife and cover the surface with buttercream. If the cakes are a little dry, sprinkle them with a few drops of sweet sherry or orange juice.

Cutting the Tops Level

Many cakes and cupcakes form a small peak while baking. However, some methods of decorating cakes require a flat surface, so, for these, trim the tops level with a knife. You can also coat cupcakes with apricot glaze and press on a disc of almond paste or sugarpaste to give a flat surface to decorate (*see* pages 40 and 46).

Storing Cakes

Chocolate and Madeira cakes can be made ahead of time and will store well for up to 5 days before decorating. Cover in fresh baking parchment, then wrap in foil and keep in a cool place, or, alternatively, freeze for up to 2 months.

Rich fruit cakes should be stored before cutting and need at least 1 month for the flavour to mature. Wedding cakes should be made 3 months ahead to give them a better flavour and enable the cake to become moist enough to cut cleanly into slices. Wrap rich fruit cakes in their baking papers, then overwrap in clean baking parchment, then a double layer of foil and seal with tape. Keep the cakes in a cool place until required.

Colouring Cake Batters

Brightly coloured layers of sponge cake are attractive and eye-catching for a children's party cake and are easily achieved. Add your choice of bright paste food colouring to the cake mix

half a teaspoon at a time, remembering these colours can be quite strong, until you reach the desired colour. For a special effect, you can divide the cake mixture into two or three batches and colour each one of these differently.

It is advisable to only use paste colourings, as the liquid ones sold in bottles will tend to make the mixture go wet, and you will need a lot more of this type to achieve a deep colour.

Carving Cake into Shapes

Once you have baked and cooled your cake, you may need to cut it into shapes to create a special novelty cake. It is a good idea to draw out the shapes on greaseproof paper with a pencil, then place this pattern on top of the cake, to cut around. This is an easy way to avoid making mistakes. If you make a mistake with the cutting,however, don't worry, you can stick pieces back together with a little buttercream.

Freezing Cakes

If you are busy organising a children's party, it is a good idea to bake the cake bases ahead of time and either freeze them whole, or cut the pieces and freeze them separately. The cakes can be baked, cooled and stored in the freezer for up to 3 months ahead, then simply defrost them at room temperature for 2–3 hours.

It is easier to cut and decorate half-frozen cake, as it is firm and will not crumble easily. You can also cover the half-frozen pieces with buttercream easily, as the crumbs will not come off the solid pieces.

∾ Freezing finished whole cakes – Completed cakes covered in basic buttercream can be frozen whole without any extra decorations. Sugarpaste-covered cakes will not freeze well, however, as the sugarpaste will start to go wet and limp when it is defrosted. Avoid freezing cakes with any extra decorations such as granulated sugar, liquorice trimmings or sweets, as the colours from these will start to bleed into the buttercream.

Basic Recipes

Rich Chocolate Cake

Square Cake Size	13 cm/5 inch square	18 cm/7 inch square	23 cm/9 inch square
Round Cake Size	15 cm/6 inch round	20 cm/8 inch round	25 cm/10 inch round
plain chocolate	50 g/2 oz	125 g/4 oz	225 g/8 oz
soft dark brown sugar	150 g/5 oz	275 g/10 oz	575 g/1^1/$_4$ lb 3oz
milk	135 ml/4^1/$_2$ fl oz	200 ml/7 fl oz	500 ml/18 fl oz
butter, softened	50 g/2 oz	125 g/4 oz	225 g/8 oz
eggs, beaten	1	3	6
plain flour	125 g/4 oz	225 g/8 oz	450 g/1 lb
bicarbonate of soda	^{1}/$_2$ tsp	1 tsp	2 tsp
Cooking time	45 mins	1 hour	1^1/$_2$ hours

Preheat the oven to 180°C/350°F/Gas Mark 4. Grease and line the tin with nonstick baking parchment. Break the chocolate into small pieces and place in a heavy-based pan with one third of the sugar and all of the milk. Heat gently until the chocolate has melted, then remove from the heat and cool.

Beat the butter and remaining sugar together until fluffy, then beat in the eggs a little at a time. Gradually beat in the cold melted chocolate mixture. Sift the flour and bicarbonate of soda into the mixture and fold together with a large metal spoon until smooth. Bake for the time shown on the chart or until a skewer inserted into the centre comes out clean. Cool for 10 minutes, then turn out of the tin onto a wire rack to cool. Store wrapped in foil until needed, or freeze wrapped tightly in foil for up to 3 months.

Madeira Cake

Square Cake Size	13 cm/5 inch square	16 cm/6 inch square	18 cm/7 inch square
Round Cake Size	15 cm/6 inch round	18 cm/7 inch round	20 cm/8 inch round
butter, softened	175 g/6 oz	225 g/8 oz	350 g/12 oz
caster sugar	175 g/6 oz	225 g/8 oz	350 g/12 oz
self-raising flour	175 g/6 oz	225 g/8 oz	350 g/12 oz
plain flour	75 g/3 oz	125 g/4 oz	175 g/6 oz
eggs	3	4	6
vanilla extract	$1/2$ tsp	1 tsp	1 tsp
glycerine	1 tsp	1 tsp	1 tsp
Cooking time	1 hour	$1-1^1/4$ hours	$1^1/4-1^1/2$ hours

Square Cake Size	20 cm/8 inch square	23 cm/9 inch square
Round Cake Size	23 cm/9 inch round	25 cm/10 inch round
butter, softened	450 g/1 lb	500 g/1 lb 2 oz
caster sugar	450 g/1 lb	500 g/1 lb 2 oz
self-raising flour	450 g/1 lb	500 g/1 lb 2 oz
plain flour	225 g/8 oz	250 g/9 oz
eggs	8	9
vanilla extract	2 tsp	1 tbsp
glycerine	2 tsp	1 tbsp
Cooking time	$1^1/2 - 1^3/4$ hours	$1^1/2 - 1^3/4$ hours

Preheat the oven to 160°C/325°F/Gas Mark 3. Grease and line the tin with nonstick baking parchment.

Cream the butter and caster sugar together in a large bowl until light and fluffy. Sift the flours together. Whisk the eggs into the mixture one at a time, adding a teaspoon of flour with each addition to prevent the mixture from curdling.

Add the remaining flour, the vanilla extract and glycerine to the mixture and fold together with a large metal spoon until the mixture is smooth.

Spoon into the tin and bake for the time shown on the chart until firm and well risen and a skewer inserted into the centre comes out clean.

Leave to cool in the tin for 10 minutes, then turn out onto a wire rack to cool. Wrap in foil and store for up to 3 days before decorating. Freeze wrapped in foil for up to 2 months.

∞ Bowl Shaped – To cook the cake in a 2 litre/3¹/₂ pint ovenproof bowl, grease the bowl well and use the amounts for the 13 cm/5 inch square cake, baking for 45 minutes–1 hour.

∞ Lemon Variation – To make the lemon variation of the Madeira cake, you can simply omit the vanilla extract and add the same amount of finely grated lemon zest.

∞ Almond Variation – To make the almond variation of the Madeira cake, you can simply omit the vanilla extract and add the same amount of almond extract.

Basic Recipes

All-in-one Quick-mix Sponge

To make sure you end up with the correct quantity of mixture for your tin when making an all-in-one sponge mix, use the guidelines below to select the ingredient quantities depending on tin size and shape.

Tin size and shape	Two 18 cm/7 inch sandwich tins	Two 20 cm/8 inch sandwich tins
Caster sugar	125 g/4 oz	175 g/6 oz
Soft tub margarine	125 g/4 oz	175 g/6 oz
Eggs	2	3
Self-raising flour	125 g/4 oz	175 g/6 oz
Baking powder	1 tsp	1 tsp
Vanilla extract	½ tsp	1 tsp
Baking time	25–30 mins	30–35 mins

Tin size and shape	13 cm/5 inch square	16 cm/6 inch square
Tin size and shape	15 cm/6 inch round	18 cm/7 inch round
Caster sugar	125 g/4 oz	175 g/6 oz
Soft tub margarine	125 g/4 oz	175 g/6 oz
Eggs	2	3
Self-raising flour	125 g/4 oz	175 g/6 oz
Baking powder	1 tsp	1 tsp
Vanilla extract	½ tsp	1 tsp
Baking time	30–35 mins	35–40 mins

Tin size and shape	18 cm/7 inch square	20 cm/8 inch square
Tin size and shape	20 cm/8 inch round	23 cm/9 inch round
Caster sugar	225 g/8 oz	350 g/12 oz
Soft tub margarine	225 g/8 oz	350 g/12 oz
Eggs	4	6
Self-raising flour	225 g/8 oz	350 g/12 oz
Baking powder	1½ tsp	2 tsp
Vanilla extract	1 tsp	2 tsp
Baking time	45–55 mins	50–60 mins

Tin size and shape	28 x 18 x 4 cm/11 x 7 x 1½ inch slab cake	30 x 25 x 5 cm/12 x 10 x 2 inch slab cake
Caster sugar	175 g/6 oz	275 g/10 oz
Soft tub margarine	175 g/6 oz	275 g/10 oz
Eggs	3	5
Self-raising flour	175 g/6 oz	275 g/10 oz
Baking powder	1 tsp	2 tsp
Vanilla extract	1 tsp	2 tsp
Baking time	30–40 mins	50–60 mins

Preheat the oven to 160°C/325°F/Gas Mark 3. Grease and line the tin with nonstick baking parchment, or butter the pudding basins well.

Place the sugar, margarine and eggs in a large mixing bowl. Sift in the flour and baking powder and add the vanilla extract.

Basic Recipes

Pudding basin size	900 ml/1½ pint	1.1 litre/2 pint
Caster sugar	125 g/4 oz	175 g/6 oz
Soft tub margarine	125 g/4 oz	175 g/6 oz
Eggs	2	3
Self-raising flour	125 g/ 4 oz	175 g/6 oz
Baking powder	1 tsp	1 tsp
Vanilla extract	½ tsp	1 tsp
Baking time	50 mins	1 hour

Beat the ingredients together with an electric mixer for 1–2 minutes until they are smooth and well combined. Spoon into the tins or basin and bake according to the time guideline above or until the cake appears well risen, just firm to the touch and is beginning to shrink away from the sides of the tin or basin.

Cool in the tin for 4 minutes, then turn out onto a wire rack to cool. Peel away the papers while still warm.

For variations:

- Chocolate Variation – Omit the vanilla extract and add 1 tbsp softened cocoa powder for the 2-egg mix, 1½ tbsp for the 3-egg mix, 2 tbsp for the 4-egg mix and 3 tbsp for the 5-egg mix.

- Orange or Lemon Variation – Omit the vanilla extract and add 2 tsp finely grated orange or lemon zest for the 2-egg mix, 3 tsp for the 3-egg mix, 4 tsp for the 4-egg mix and 2 tbsp for the 5-egg mix.

- Coffee Variation – Omit the vanilla extract and add 1 tbsp coffee essence for the 2-egg mix, 1½ tbsp for the 3-egg mix, 2 tbsp for the 4-egg mix and 2½ tbsp for the 5-egg mix.

Basic Vanilla Cupcakes

Makes 12–14

125 g/4 oz caster sugar
125 g/4 oz soft tub margarine
2 medium eggs
125 g/4 oz self-raising flour
½ tsp baking powder
½ tsp vanilla extract

Preheat the oven to 190°C/375°F/Gas Mark 5.
Line a bun tray with paper cases.

Place all the cupcake ingredients in a large bowl
and beat with an electric mixer for about 2 minutes
until light and smooth. Fill the paper cases halfway
up with the mixture. Bake for about 15 minutes
until firm, risen and golden.

Remove to a wire rack to cool. Keep for 2–3 days in an
airtight container. Can be frozen for up to 2 months, but the
paper cases will come away when thawed and these will
need replacing.

- Chocolate Variation – Omit the caster sugar and use soft light brown sugar
  instead. Sift 25 g/1 oz cocoa powder in with the flour and baking powder. Omit the
  vanilla extract and add 2 tbsp milk instead. Mix and bake as above.

- Cherry & Almond Variation – Add 50 g/2 oz finely chopped washed glacé cherries.
  Omit the vanilla extract and use almond extract instead. Mix and bake as above.

Special Requirements

~

If you have to cater for a child who has an allergy to wheat or dairy products, there are substitutes that can be baked into a cake for a special occasion.

∾ Flour – Packs of both plain and self-raising wheat-free and gluten-free flours for baking can now be purchased in supermarkets and health-food stores. Make sure you check the sell-by dates on these flours, however, as they do not last as long as normal flours and will start to deteriorate.

∾ Xanthan Gum – This special ingredient is a natural product that is needed in gluten- and wheat-free baking to stabilise cakes and stop them from crumbling. Some flours contain a small amount of xanthan gum, but extra is needed, according to the recipe instructions, for success.

∾ Fats – Dairy-free sunflower spread or soya spread can be used as a substitute for butter and margarine in baking.

∾ Milks and Creams – Dairy-free milks can be used for baking, such as soya, almond and rice milk. Soya whipping cream, a blend of vegetable fat and soya beans, can also be used for baking. Coconut cream, sold in cartons, can be whipped to a texture similar to double cream and folded together with icing sugar to make an alternative frosting.

Gluten-free Sponge

Serves 8–10

250 g/9oz dairy-free spread
250 g/9 oz golden caster sugar
4 large eggs
½ tsp vanilla extract
2 tbsp almond milk
225 g/8 oz gluten-free self-raising flour
1½ tsp gluten-free baking powder
1 tsp xanthan gum
40 g/1½ oz ground almonds

Preheat the oven to 190°C/375°F/Gas Mark 5. Grease two
20 cm/8 inch sandwich tins and line the bases with nonstick
baking parchment.

Place the dairy-free spread in a bowl with the sugar and whisk
with an electric mixer until light and fluffy. Whisk the eggs, vanilla
and almond milk together, then gradually add to the mixture in
the bowl and whisk until smooth.

Sift the flour, baking powder, xanthan gum and ground
almonds together, then fold into the mixture in the bowl.
Spoon into the tins and smooth the tops level. Bake for
about 20 minutes until golden and the sides begin to shrink
away from the tins.

Leave in the tins for 5 minutes, then turn out onto wire racks to cool. Sandwich together with frosting
made with dairy-free spread and icing sugar or jam.

Special Requirements

Decorating
Basics

Giving cakes and cupcakes that all-important decorative touch is not always as easy as it looks! With key information on decorating ingredients, equipment and techniques, reading this section will help your masterpieces to look as good as possible. Also included are extremely useful icing recipes, including buttercream frosting, cream cheese frosting, sugarpaste icing and flower paste, which will feature in many of the projects throughout this book.

Decorating Ingredients

༄

There are a multitude of ingredients you can use to decorate your cakes. Below, you will find reference to many of the icings, colourings and edible decorations you can buy, as well as, later, key icing recipes, which will show you how to whip up your own icings from scratch. The basic icing recipes will be referenced often throughout the main recipe chapters.

- **Icing Sugar** – Icing sugar is fine and powdery. It is usually sold plain and white, but can also be bought as an unrefined golden (or 'natural') variety. Use it for delicate icings, frostings and decorations. Store this sugar in a dry place, as it can absorb moisture and this will make it go hard and lumpy. Always sift this sugar at least once, or preferably twice, before you use it, to remove any hard lumps that would prevent icing from achieving a smooth texture – lumpy icing is impossible to pipe out.

- **Fondant Icing Sugar** – This is sold in plain and flavoured varieties and gives a beautiful glossy finish to cake toppings. Just add a little boiled water to the sugar, according to the packet instructions, to make a shiny icing that can be poured or drizzled over cake tops to give a very professional finish. Colour the plain white icing with a few spots of paste food colouring to achieve your desired result.

Flavoured fondant icing sugar is sold in strawberry, raspberry, orange, lemon and blackcurrant flavours and also has colouring added. These sugars are ideal if you want to make a large batch of cakes with different-coloured and -flavoured toppings. Flavoured fondant sugars can also be whisked with softened unsalted butter and cream cheese to make delicious frostings in just a few moments.

- **Royal Icing Sugar** – Royal icing sets to a classic, firm Christmas-cake-style covering or can be made to a softer consistency to give a glossy finish. Sold in packs as plain white sugar, this is whisked with cold water to give an instant royal icing. It has dried egg white included in the mixture, so does not need the long beating that traditional royal icing recipes require. It is also ideal to use for those who cannot eat raw egg whites.

- **Tubes of Writing Icing** – You can buy small tubes of ready-coloured royal icing or gel icing, usually in sets of black, red, yellow and blue, and these are ideal for small amounts of writing or for piping on dots or small decorations.

- **Food Colourings** – You can buy food colourings in liquid, paste, gel and powder or dust forms in a great range of colours.

Paste food colourings are best for using with sugarpaste. These are sold in small tubs and are very concentrated, so should be added to the sugarpaste dot by dot on the end of a wooden cocktail stick. Knead the colouring in evenly, adding more until you get the colour you require.

Liquid and gel food colourings are ideal for adding to frostings. Add this cautiously, drop by drop, beating the frosting well until you reach the colour you require.

Dusts, sprays and lustre colourings should be lightly brushed onto dry sugarpaste with a paintbrush to form a delicate sheen to decorations such as flowers. Liquid paint and spray-on metallic colourings add a glossy sheen effect to decorations.

Coloured sugars can be made by adding a few dots of paste colouring to granulated sugar with a toothpick. Coloured sugars add sparkle to the sides of cakes and cupcakes. Coloured sugars can make up the background of a children's novelty cake, such the sand in a seaside cake, or a sparkly topping.

- **Bought Sugar Decorations and Sprinkles** – A range of sprinkles can be bought in supermarkets or by mail order from specialist cake-decorating companies.

Decorating Ingredients

Apricot Glaze Almond Paste

Makes 450 g/1 lb to cover
2 x 20 cm/8 inch, round
cakes, or 24 small cakes

For the Apricot Glaze:

450 g/1 lb apricot jam
3 tbsp water
1 tsp lemon juice

For the Almond Paste:

125 g/4 oz sifted icing sugar
125 g/4 oz caster sugar
225 g/8 oz ground almonds
1 medium egg
1 tsp lemon juice

For the Apricot Glaze, place the jam, water and juice in a heavy-based saucepan and heat gently, stirring, until soft and melted. Boil rapidly for 1 minute, then press through a fine sieve with the back of a wooden spoon. Discard the pieces of fruit. Use immediately for glazing or sticking on almond paste, or pour into a clean jar or airtight plastic container and store in the refrigerator for up to 3 months.

For the Almond Paste, stir the sugars and ground almonds together in a bowl. Whisk the egg and lemon juice together and mix into the dry ingredients. Knead until the paste is smooth. Wrap tightly in clingfilm or foil to keep airtight and store in the refrigerator until needed. The paste can be made 2–3 days ahead of time, but, after that, it will start to dry out and become difficult to handle.

To use the paste, knead on a surface dusted with icing sugar. Brush the top of the cake(s) with apricot glaze. Roll out the paste to a circle large enough to cover the cake, or cut out discs large enough to cover the tops of the cupcakes. Press onto the cakes. To cover the sides of a large cake, cut out a strip long enough to go round the cake (work out the length by measuring the circumference with string). Roll the paste up into a coil and press one end onto the side of the cake. Unroll the paste, pressing into the cake as you go round. Press the top and sides together to join. Smooth the top and sides and leave to dry out for 24 hours before icing.

Basic Buttercream Frosting

Covers a 20 cm/8 inch,
round cake,
or 12 small cakes

Ingredients

150 g/5 oz unsalted butter,
softened at room temperature
225 g/8 oz icing sugar, sifted
2 tbsp hot milk or water
1 tsp vanilla extract
food colourings of choice

Beat the butter until light and fluffy, then beat in the sifted icing sugar and hot milk or water in two batches.

Add the vanilla extract and any colourings. Store chilled for up to 2 days in an airtight container.

Variations
Omit the vanilla extract and instead:

- Coffee – Blend 2 tsp coffee extract with the milk.

- Chocolate – Blend 2 tbsp cocoa powder to a paste with 2 tbsp boiling water and use instead of the hot milk or water.

- Lemon – Beat in 1 tbsp fresh lemon juice, sieved.

Cream Cheese Frosting

Covers a 20 cm/8 inch, round cake, or 12 small cakes

Ingredients

50 g/2 oz unsalted butter, softened
at room temperature
300 g/11 oz icing sugar, sifted
flavourings of choice
food colourings of choice
125 g/4 oz full-fat cream cheese

Beat the butter and icing sugar together until light and fluffy.

Add flavourings and colourings of choice and beat again.

Add the cream cheese and whisk until light and fluffy.

Do not overbeat, however, as the mixture can become runny.

Sugarpaste Icing
(a.k.a. Fondant for Rolling or Modelling)

Makes 350 g/12 oz to cover a
20 cm/8 inch, round cake,
or 12 small cakes, or use
for decorations

Ingredients

1 medium egg white
1 tbsp liquid glucose
350 g/12 oz icing sugar, sifted,
plus extra for dusting

Place the egg white and liquid glucose in a large mixing bowl
and stir together, breaking up the egg white.

Add the icing sugar gradually, mixing in until the mixture
binds together and forms a ball.

Turn the ball of icing out onto a clean surface dusted with
icing sugar and knead for 5 minutes until soft but firm enough
to roll out.

If the icing is too soft, knead in a little more icing sugar until
the mixture is pliable.

To colour, knead in paste food colouring. Do not use liquid
food colouring, as this is not suitable and will make the
sugarpaste limp.

To use, roll out thinly on a clean surface dusted with icing
sugar to a circle large enough to cover a cake, or cut out
discs large enough to cover the top of each cupcake.

Flower Paste

Ingredients

2 tsp powdered gelatine
2 tsp liquid glucose
2 tsp white vegetable fat
450 g/1 lb sifted icing sugar
1 tsp gum tragacanth powder
1 egg white
icing sugar, for dusting

Flower, petal or 'gum' paste is used for making very thin, delicate flowers and decorations, which set hard so that they can be handled easily.

Flower paste will roll out much more thinly than sugarpaste and is worth using for wedding cakes, as it gives a realistic finish to flowers, and these can be made ahead of time and easily stored. It can be bought from cake decorating suppliers or by mail order in small, ready-made slabs in different colours or as a powder that can be reconstituted with a little cold water and made into a paste.

To make your own, follow the recipe and store the paste in the refrigerator, tightly wrapped in strong plastic until needed.

Place 1^1/$_2$ tsp cold water in a heatproof bowl. Sprinkle over the gelatine and add the liquid glucose and white fat. Place the bowl over a saucepan of hot water and heat until melted, stirring occasionally. Cool slightly.

Sift the icing sugar and gum tragacanth powder into a bowl, make a well in the centre and add the egg white and the cooled gelatine mixture. Mix together to make a soft paste.

Knead the paste on a surface dusted with icing sugar until smooth, then wrap in clingfilm to exclude all air. Leave for 2 hours, then break off small pieces and use to make fine flowers and petals.

Royal Icing

Makes 500 g/1 lb 2 oz to
cover a 20 cm/8 inch,
round cake,
or 12 small cakes

Ingredients

2 medium egg whites
500 g/1 lb 2 oz icing sugar, sifted
2 tsp lemon juice

Put the egg whites in a large bowl and whisk lightly with
a fork to break up the whites until foamy.

Sift in half the icing sugar with the lemon juice and beat
well with an electric mixer for 4 minutes, or by hand with
a wooden spoon for about 10 minutes, until smooth.

Gradually sift in the remaining icing sugar and beat
again until thick, smooth and brilliant white and the icing
forms soft peaks when flicked up with a spoon.

Keep the royal icing covered with a clean, damp cloth
until ready for use, or store in the refrigerator in an
airtight plastic container until needed.

If making royal icing to use later, beat it again before
use to remove any air bubbles that may have formed in
the mixture.

Glacé Icing

Covers a 20 cm/8 inch, round cake (top), or 12 small cakes

Ingredients

225 g/8 oz icing sugar
few drops lemon juice, or vanilla
or almond extract
2–3 tbsp boiling water
liquid or paste
food colouring (optional)

Sift the icing sugar into a bowl and add the chosen flavouring, then gradually stir in enough water to mix to the consistency of thick cream.

Beat with a wooden spoon until the icing is thick enough to coat the back of the spoon, and add a few drops of liquid or paste food colouring, if desired. Use immediately, as the icing will begin to form a skin as it starts to set.

Decorating Equipment

c

If you are to produce the best results possible, sugarcraft and cake decorating require a fair few more pieces of equipment than standard baking!

∾ **Cake Boards** – Thin and thicker drum-style boards are needed to give the cakes a good base.

∾ **Dowels** – Cake dowels are small, short pieces of thin plastic or wood that are used to support tiers of cake. Four dowels are usually inserted into a cake base at equal distances, to support the next layer placed on top.

∾ **Turntable** – A heavy-based icing turntable helps you coat the sides of a cake easily.

∾ **Plastic Rolling Pins** – A long plastic rolling pin is needed for easy rolling out of sugarpaste. Wooden pins can be used for almond paste, but are not good for sugarpaste, which tends to stick to them. A small plastic rolling pin is useful for rolling out small quantities of flower paste.

∾ **Boards** – Large plastic boards are useful if you do not have a nonstick kitchen surface and small plastic boards are vital for rolling out small pieces of flower paste.

∾ **Brushes** – A selection of fine-tipped paintbrushes should be kept just for adding painted-on details and dusting lustre powders onto sugarpaste projects.

∾ **Wooden Toothpicks** – Toothpicks are used for colouring, rolling and fluting scraps of flower paste, and lifting delicate pieces of sugarpaste into position.

- Scissors – A separate small pair of sharp, pointed scissors is needed for cutting out templates, snipping into sugarpaste and shaping with the pointed ends.

- Smoothers – Smoothers are essential for achieving a smooth finish on a sugarpaste-covered cake. Holding one in each hand will give a perfect top and sides to a cake.

- Spirit Level – A spirit level is needed for tiered cakes such as wedding cakes, to check that the levels are even and correct.

- Garlic or Icing Press – A press is used to achieve long strands of sugarpaste – for hair or grass, for example.

- Wooden Spoon Handles and Spaghetti – Use wooden spoon handles wrapped in clingfilm for shaping ribbons and bows. Use short pieces of spaghetti for shaping difficult small areas.

- Tweezers – A pair of tweezers is useful for positioning small, delicate items, or making a rough pattern in sugarpaste.

- Silicone Moulds – These are small moulds made in the shape of flowers, leaves, lace, etc. that can be filled with flower paste, which is then pushed out to give an instant shaped decoration.

- Stamps and Cutters – Cutters for cutting out intricate icing shapes can be bought from specialist cake and baking stores. Like normal cookie cutters, they

Decorating Equipment

come in classic metal styles, in plastic, or as plunger-style stamps. If you do not have appropriate cutters, there are some templates at the back of this book that can be used instead.

You will need a selection of flower cutters and stamps made from plastic or metal to cut out petals, blossom and leaves from flower paste. A good basic selection will include small, medium and large blossom cutters, a selection of daisy, star flowers and Tudor rose cutters and some basic petal and leaf cutters.

∾ Small Plastic Bottles – Small, reusable plastic storage bottles with pointed tips are handy for keeping different colours of royal icing for piping onto cakes.

∾ Ribbons – Satin or floristry paper ribbons give each cake a flourish and can cover over mistakes or defects.

∾ Print Wrap – Patterns can be printed on edible paper or rice paper. Edible printed ribbons can be bought from cake-decorating specialists.

∾ Edible-ink Pens – Small, felt-tipped pens, loaded with food colouring are useful for marking faces or tiny details onto sugarpaste models.

Sugarpaste Tools

∾ Balling Tool – A balling tool (top right) is invaluable for making rounded shapes and impressions.

- **Boning Tool** – A boning tool (right, second from top) has a large and a smaller rounded and curved end. These will help you to model hollow shapes in balls of sugarpaste, or curved cup shapes in petals and flowers.

- **Fluting Tool** – A fluting tool (right, third from top) creates open centres in cut-out shapes.

- **Scriber Needle** – A scriber needle or pin tool (right, fourth from top) is used for marking out lettering or patterns on your cake.

- **Quilting Tool** – A quilting tool is needed for straight lines and stitching effects.

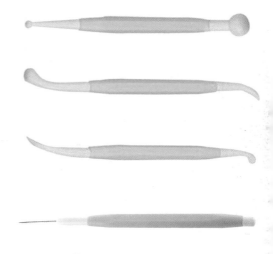

- **Cutting Wheel** – This is used for cutting sugarpaste and flower paste in a wide variety of patterns. You can use a crimped-edge pasta-cutting wheel for a crimped effect.

- **Crimping Tools** – Operated like tweezers, crimpers with different edges give finishes such as heart shapes, curved swags and quilted-line effects, often around the edge of a cake.

- **Flower Nail** – A flower nail (bottom right in the picture on the right) is used for making piped royal icing or buttercream flowers. A square of waxed paper is attached to the 'head' of the 'nail' and the nail is turned as the petals are piped out onto the paper.

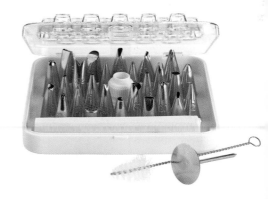

Decorating Equipment

Piping Bags and Nozzles

∞ **Fabric Bags** – A nylon piping bag that comes with a set of five nozzles is a very useful piece of equipment for decorating with icings. Look for a set with a plain nozzle and various star nozzles for piping swirls. The larger the star nozzle, the wider the swirls will be on the finished cake. Nylon piping bags can be washed out in warm soapy water and dried out, ready to reuse again and again.

∞ **Disposable Bags** – Paper or clear plastic icing bags are available and are quick and easy to use. Clear plastic piping bags are useful for piping large swirls on cupcakes.

∞ **Make a Paper Icing Bag** – Cut out a 38 x 25.5 cm/ 15 x 10 inch rectangle of greaseproof paper. Fold it diagonally in half to form two triangular shapes. Cut along the fold line to make two triangles. One of these triangles can be used another time – it is quicker and easier to make two at a time from one square than to measure and mark out a triangle on a sheet of paper.

Fold one of the points on the long side of the triangle over the top to make a sharp cone and hold in the centre. Fold the other sharp end of the triangle over the cone. Hold all the points together at the back of the cone, keeping the pointed end sharp. Turn the points inside the top edge, fold over to make a crease, then secure with a piece of sticky tape.

To use, snip away the end, place a piping nozzle in position and fill the bag with icing, or fill the bag with icing first, then snip away a tiny hole at the end for piping a plain edge, writing or piping tiny dots.

Decorating Techniques

ℰ

Using Buttercream and Cream Cheese Frostings

These soft icings can be swirled onto the tops of cakes with a small palette knife or placed in a piping bag fitted with a star nozzle to pipe impressive whirls, such as when you want to finish off your cake with a piped border or simply add those elegant flourishes.

Keep cakes with frostings in a cool place, or refrigerate, as they contain a high percentage of butter, which will melt easily in too warm a place.

- **Covering a Cake with Frosting** – Do not be mean with the amount of frosting you use. If this is scraped on thinly, you will see the cake underneath, so be generous.

If your cake has a dark crumb base, such as a chocolate cake, place it in the freezer for 15 minutes before spreading over the buttercream, to give a firm base that will keep the crumbs from spreading into the buttercream.

Place a generous amount in the centre of the cake and spread this over the top with a large, flat-bladed knife or a palette knife. Spread over the sides separately and tidy up the edges with an icing scraper.

- **Piping Buttercream onto Cupcakes** – Take a large piping bag and add the nozzle of your choice. A star nozzle will give a whirly effect and a plain nozzle will create a smooth, coiled effect. Half-fill the bag, shake down the buttercream and fill the bag again. Twist the top round to seal tightly. Squeeze the bag until the buttercream comes out. Start on the outer edge and gently squeeze the buttercream out in one continuous spiral. Lift the bag away to give a peaked finish to the top.

- **Decorating Buttercream** – Cakes coated in buttercream can be decorated easily with colourful sprinkles and sugars. This is easy with cupcakes. Place the sprinkles in a small saucer or on a piece of nonstick baking parchment and roll the outside edges of each cupcake in the decorations.

Using Sugarpaste

Sugarpaste is a versatile icing, as it can be used for covering whole cakes or modelling all sorts of fancy decorations.

- Paste food colourings are best for working with sugarpaste and a little goes a very long way. As these are very concentrated, use a cocktail stick to add dots of paste gradually, until you are sure of the colour, and knead in until even.

- Always roll out almond paste or sugarpaste on a surface lightly dusted with icing sugar. Use cornflour for rolling out flower paste, as this needs to be kept dry and flexible.

- Leave sugarpaste-covered cakes to firm up for 2 hours before adding decorations, as this provides a good finished surface to work on.

- Once decorated, store sugarpaste-covered cakes in large boxes in a cool place. Do not store in a refrigerator, as the sugarpaste will become damp and colours may run.

Covering a Large Cake with Sugarpaste Icing

If covered in almond paste, brush the paste lightly with a little boiled water, or, if using buttercream or apricot glaze, spread these over the trimmed cake to give a surface for the sugarpaste to stick to.

Knead the sugarpaste until softened, then roll into a ball. Roll out to about 1 cm/¹/₂ inch thickness on a flat surface lightly dusted with icing sugar, moving the sugarpaste occasionally to prevent it from sticking to the surface.

Take a piece of string and measure the distance across the top and down either side of the cake and cut the sugarpaste 2.5 cm/1 inch larger in order to cover the whole cake. Lift the sugarpaste carefully onto the cake, holding it flat with your palms until it is central.

Dust your hands with icing sugar and smooth the icing down over the top and sides of the cake, fluting out the bottom edges. Do not pleat the icing, as this will leave lines. Smooth down to remove any air bubbles under the surface of the icing, then trim the edges with a sharp knife.

Using the flat of your hand or an icing smoother, flatten out the top and sides using a circular movement. Do not wear any rings, as these will leave ridges in the soft icing. Gather up the trimmings into a ball and keep these tightly wrapped in a plastic bag.

To Cover Cupcakes

Cut out circles the size of the cupcake tops. Coat each cake with a little apricot glaze or buttercream and press on the circles to form a flat surface.

To Copy Patterns from the Templates onto Sugarpaste

At the back of this book, you will find templates for some of the shapes used in the recipes. Trace the pattern you want onto a sheet of clear greaseproof paper or nonstick baking parchment. Roll out the sugarpaste thinly, then position the traced pattern on top. Mark over the pattern with the tip of a small, sharp knife or a pin. Remove the paper and cut out the marked-on pattern with a small, sharp knife.

∾ Making Flat Decorations

To make letters, numbers or flat decorations, roll out the sugarpaste thinly and cut out the shapes. Leave to dry on nonstick baking parchment on a flat surface or a tray for 2–3 hours to make them firm and easy to handle.

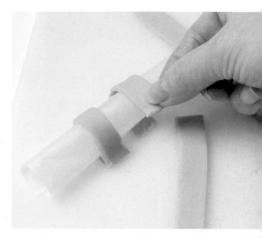

∾ Making Bows

Roll out the sugarpaste thinly on a surface lightly dusted with icing sugar and, with a knife, cut out long, thin, narrow strips.

Roll small squares of baking parchment into narrow tubes, or line the handle of a wooden spoon with clingfilm. Fold the icing over the paper or handle to form loops and leave to dry and harden for 2 hours, then carefully remove the paper or spoon handle.

To make bows that are placed directly onto the cake, fill the centre of each loop with cotton wool balls, then remove these when the icing is firm.

∾ Making Roses

Colour the sugarpaste icing with pink paste food colouring. Take a small piece of sugarpaste and make a small cone shape, then roll a small pea-size piece of sugarpaste into a ball. Flatten out the ball into a petal shape and wrap this round the cone shape.

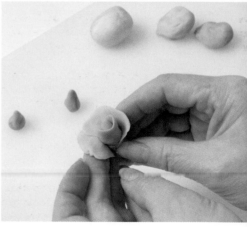

Continue adding more petals (*see* picture, right), then trim the thick base. Leave to dry for 2 hours in a clean egg box lined with foil or clingfilm.

❧   Decorating Techniques

Making Lilies – Lilies of all sizes can make elegant decorations for cakes.

Colour a little sugarpaste a deep yellow and mould this into thin sausage shapes. Leave these to firm on nonstick baking parchment or clingfilm for 2 hours.

Thinly roll out white sugarpaste and mark out small squares of 4 x 4 cm/1½ x 1½ inches. Wrap each square round a yellow centre to form a lily (*see* picture, top left) and press the ends together. Place the lilies on nonstick baking parchment to dry out for 2 hours.

Making Daisies – Daisies of all sizes are a popular flower to be found on decorated cakes.

To model from sugarpaste, roll out a little sugarpaste thinly and, using a daisy stamp, press out small flower shapes and mould these into a curve.

Leave the daisies to dry out on nonstick baking parchment, then pipe dots into the centre of each one with yellow royal icing or a small tube of gel writing icing.

Making Butterfly Wings – Colour the sugarpaste and roll out thinly. Trace round butterfly patterns (e.g. page 249) and cut out shapes. Leave these to dry flat on nonstick baking parchment for 4 hours to make them firm and easy to lift.

Making Ruffles – To make frills and ruffles, roll out the sugarpaste on a surface lightly dusted with icing sugar and stamp out a fluted circle 6 cm/2½ inches wide with a pastry cutter.

Cut away a small plain disc 2.5 cm/1 inch wide from the centre, and discard. Take a cocktail stick and roll this back and forth until the sugarpaste begins to frill up.

∾ **Using Silicone Moulds** – Push-up silicone moulds have made cake decorating so easy, as all you have to do is press a little sugarpaste into the mould and then press this out and you will have a beautiful ready-made decoration. You can buy these moulds online from sugarcraft specialists or from hobby and craft shops. You will find a huge selection in all sorts of shapes and sizes – flowers, borders, buttons, toys and novelties of all types.

To make a moulded shape, roll out a pea-size ball of sugarpaste on a surface dusted with icing sugar until pliable. Make sure the mould is clean and dry and dust it with a little icing sugar. Gently push the paste into the mould. Don't force it too hard or it will clog the mould. Turn the mould over and flex it until the sugarpaste shape drops out. Repeat until you have the number of shapes needed, then leave these to dry out overnight on a sheet of nonstick baking parchment.

∾ **Using Embossing Tools and Mats to Decorate** – Embossing tools make lacy impressions and designs on sugarpaste. These come as stamps or plastic strips with a raised impression and are pushed into the soft paste to make the pattern. They can be used in conjunction with lustre powders to make a two-tone effect.

Decorating Techniques

Using Royal Icing

To pipe royal icing borders, fit a small paper icing bag with a star or a straight nozzle and fill the bag three-quarters full with royal icing. Fold over the top and push out a little of the icing at right angles to the base of the cake. As the icing is pushed out, reduce the pressure and lift the bag away. Continue piping another shape next to the first one, until you have completed the border round the base of the cake. You can use the same technique for piping buttercream onto cakes, but this will be a little softer to pipe out and requires less pressure.

Using Glacé Icing

A quick and easy way to cover cakes is by using glacé icing. This is just a paste made by mixing icing sugar and water until a coating consistency is formed. Liquid or paste food colourings can be added to glacé and it needs to be used immediately, as it will start to set quickly. Add any sprinkles or decorations to the wet glacé icing immediately, or sprinkle over chopped nuts or cherries.

To make a feathered effect in glacé icing, colour one batch of icing, then colour a little icing in a contrasting colour and place this in a small paper icing bag. Spread the main colour over the cake and then pipe a pattern onto the wet icing and pull a wooden toothpick through this immediately to give a feathered effect. Work quickly while the icing is wet and then leave to dry and set for 1 hour.

Using Chocolate

～ **Melting Chocolate** – Care and attention is needed to melt chocolate for baking and cake-decorating needs. If the chocolate gets too hot or comes into contact with water or steam, it will 'seize' or stiffen and form into a hard ball instead of a smooth melted mixture. You can add a little vegetable oil or margarine, a teaspoon at a time, to the mixture to make it liquid again.

To melt chocolate, break the bar into small pieces, or grate or chop it, and place in a heatproof bowl standing over a bowl of warm, not hot, water. Make sure the bowl containing the chocolate is completely dry and that steam or water cannot enter the bowl. Heat the water to a gentle simmer only and leave the bowl to stand for about 5 minutes. Do not let the water get too hot or the chocolate will reach too high a temperature and will lose its sheen.

The microwave oven is ideal for melting chocolate. Place the chocolate pieces in a small microwave-proof bowl and melt gently on low or defrost settings in small bursts of 30 seconds, checking and stirring in between, until the chocolate has melted.

Covering Cupcakes with Melted Chocolate – If the cakes have domed, trim them neatly. While the chocolate is still warm, pour a little over each cupcake. Take each cake and gently tap on a surface to spread the icing to the edges of the cases. Add sprinkles or decorations and leave to set for 1 hour.

Covering a Cake with Chocolate – Trim the cake level if necessary, then place on a wire rack over a tray. Pour the warm melted chocolate over and, working quickly, spread the chocolate over the top and sides with a palette knife. Patch up any bare areas and leave to set for 1 hour. Add any decorations while the icing is still wet and leave to dry.

Chocolate Shapes – Spread a thin layer of melted chocolate over a cool surface, and leave until just set but not hard. Use shaped cutters or a sharp knife to cut out shapes. Use to decorate your cakes.

Decorating Techniques

Finishing Touches

You will find a huge selection of cake accessories in craft and hobby shops or online. These include edible jewels made from sugar, which add sparkle to large and small cakes. Edible pearls and diamonds can set off a wedding cake, or more fun edible jewels can be a favourite for children's party cakes.

∾ Glitter comes in bright colours in pots and is sold as dust or granules with a shine. Dusting powders give a more subtle natural sheen to flowers and ribbons.

∾ Printed Papers and Ribbons made from edible rice paper can create a pretty effect and can be cut through when serving the cake.

∾ Paper Cupcake Liners made from bright cut-out papers can be wrapped around deep cupcakes for a special occasion. Themed and patterned paper liners are also available.

∾ Ribbons and Paper Lace Trims can be found in abundance in craft and hobby shops or online cake-decorating suppliers. A colourful contrasting or toning ribbon will set off a cake beautifully. Tie ribbons round the finished cake and secure them with a dab of royal icing. Never use pins on a cake.

Stacking Tiered Cakes

For large, tiered cakes, you will need to insert small sticks of wooden or plastic dowelling into the lower tiers to take the weight of the next layer and stop it sinking.

First, decide where you need to position the dowels: cover the cake with almond paste and sugarpaste and place centrally on a board. Place a sheet of baking parchment over the cake and cut to the size of the top of the cake. Based on the size of the cake that is to stand on top, decide where you want the dowels to go and mark four equal dots in a square, centrally on the paper.

Replace the paper and mark through each dot with a skewer. Remove the paper and push a dowel down into the cake at each mark. Make a mark with a pencil on the dowel at the point where the dowel comes out of the cake. Pull the dowels out of the cake and, using a serrated knife, trim them to 1 mm/$^1/_{32}$ inch above the pencil mark. Replace the dowels in the cake and ensure these are all 1 mm above the surface of the cake. If not, trim them again, then place the next tier of the cake on top (this should be sitting on a thin cake board that fits its size). Repeat if using three tiers.

If you are going to transport a tiered cake, remember to take each tier in a separate cardboard cake box and assemble it at the venue. Do not even think of trying to transport a tiered cake once it is stacked up – it will be too heavy and you may damage all your hard work.

Seasonal ❧ Celebration

❧

Kids love celebrations, and nothing else says 'celebration' quite like a cake! Whether the occasion is Christmas, Easter, Halloween or a much-awaited birthday, make each party a celebration to remember with these stunning cakes. If you're hosting an Easter Egg Hunt party, then the Cute Creatures Easter Cupcakes are the perfect accompaniment, or for a Halloween showstopper, the Smiling Pumpkin Cake is both spooky and delicious!

Patchwork Bears Christening Cake

Serves 10–12

For the cake base:

1 x 20 cm/8 inch, round Madeira
cake (*see* page 28)
8 tbsp apricot glaze

To decorate:

1.2 kg/2 lb 10 oz ready-to-roll
sugarpaste
blue and pink paste food colourings
icing sugar, for dusting
blue ribbon trim
candles

Trim the top of the cake flat if it has peaked, then brush the apricot glaze over the top and sides. Colour 650 g/1 lb 7 oz sugarpaste pale blue and use to cover the cake (*see* page 62). Trim, then place the cake on a 25 cm/ 10 inch cake board and cover the edges of the board with the trimmings.

Colour 250 g/9 oz sugarpaste pink. Roll out 100 g/3^1/$_2$ oz of it on a surface dusted with icing sugar, then, using a cutter or the template on page 255, cut out six teddies. Stick these on top of the cake with a little cold boiled water and impress a teddy design on each with an embosser or cutter.

Roll out the remaining pink sugarpaste. Measure the depth of the cake and cut out squares of sugarpaste so that they will fit three deep. Use embossing tools or various kitchen utensils to press a variety of designs onto the pieces. Repeat with 150 g/5 oz white sugarpaste. You will need about 90 pieces altogether. Stick these around the cake with a little cold boiled water and pick out some of the designs with blue or pink colouring, thinned with a little water.

Roll out the remaining white sugarpaste and, using a lace cutter or pastry cutting wheel, cut triangles to fit around the top and bottom of the cake. Pierce each with a small flower cutter before attaching to the cake. Trim the side of the cake board with a thin blue ribbon and add matching pink and blue candles to finish.

Bows & Spots Cake

Serves 8–10

For the cake base:

1 x 15 cm/6 inch Madeira cake
(*see* page 28)

To decorate:

700 g/1½ lb ready-to-roll
sugarpaste
black and turquoise paste
food colouring
icing sugar, for dusting
½ batch vanilla buttercream

Colour 25 g/1 oz sugarpaste black and 150 g/5 oz turquoise. Roll out the turquoise sugarpaste thinly on a surface dusted with icing sugar and cut into eight strips 10 cm/4 inches long and 5 cm/2 inches wide. Fold the strips over to make loops, pinch together and leave to dry on wooden spoon handles lined with clingfilm. Repeat, rolling out 50 g/2 oz white sugarpaste to make six strips. Press an embossing tool onto the strips to make a pattern, then fold over into loops as above.

Cut the cake in half and spread one half with buttercream. Sandwich the two halves back together and spread the top and sides with the remaining buttercream. Roll out the remaining white sugarpaste on a surface lightly dusted with icing sugar to a circle large enough to cover the cake. Use to cover the cake (*see* page 62). Use a crimping tool to make a pattern around the top edge of the cake or mark with a knife. Roll out scraps of white sugarpaste and cut out a strip long enough to go around the cake, dampen with cold boiled water, then stick around the base of the cake.

Roll out the scraps of blue sugarpaste and cut out five discs, then cut the centre out of these with a small circular cutter. Mark with an embossing tool or a knife to make a pattern, then dampen the shapes and stick to the sides of the cake. Repeat with the black sugarpaste to make three black discs. Roll the black sugarpaste scraps into tiny balls and press these onto the sides of the cake at intervals to finish.

Rainbow Layers Birthday Cake

Serves 18

For the cake base:

3 batches all-in-one quick-mix
sponge batter (*see* page 30)
red, orange, yellow, green, blue
and purple paste food colourings

To decorate:

2 batches vanilla buttercream
225 g/8 oz ready-to-roll sugarpaste
coloured sprinkles
icing sugar, for dusting

Line two 20 cm/8 inch, round sandwich tins with nonstick baking parchment. Take one batch of quick-mix sponge batter, halve the mixture and colour one half red and one half orange, adding enough food colouring to give a deep tone. Bake following the instructions on page 30–32, then turn the cakes out to cool. Clean the tins and repeat, making two more sponge layers, colouring one yellow and one green. Turn the cakes out to cool and repeat the process, colouring the last two layers one blue and one purple.

When completely cool, place the purple layer on a cake stand and spread on a thin layer of buttercream. Top with a blue layer, spread another layer of buttercream over and continue spreading and layering with the green, yellow, orange and red cakes. Place a quarter of the remaining buttercream in a piping bag fitted with a star nozzle. Spread the remaining buttercream over the top and round the sides with a palette knife, then smooth round the sides of the cake with a serrated icing smoother. Pipe a shell border round the top and base of the cake and scatter coloured sprinkles over.

Colour 50 g/2 oz batches of sugarpaste blue, purple, green and orange. Roll out the colours thinly on a surface dusted with icing sugar and cut out large and small disc shapes with small round cutters. Press the discs round the sides of the cake as shown to finish.

Pretty Pink Cupcakes

Makes 12

For the cakes:

1 batch vanilla cupcakes
(*see* page 33)
2 tbsp apricot glaze

To decorate:

700 g/1¹/₂ lb ready-to-roll
sugarpaste
pink paste food colouring
icing sugar, for dusting
pink lustre powder
1 small tube or 1 tbsp royal icing
(*see* page 50)

Colour half the sugarpaste pink and leave the remainder white. Roll out a small amount of pink and white sugarpaste on a surface dusted with icing sugar and cut out six small pink daisies and six white daisies with a small daisy stamp. Make a pink centre for each one and leave to dry in empty egg boxes lined with crumpled foil. When dry, dust the centre of each one with a little pink lustre powder.

Trim the cupcakes to give them a rounded shape and brush the apricot glaze over. Roll out the remaining pink sugarpaste thinly on a board or surface dusted with icing sugar. Using a round cutter, stamp out six circles 6 cm/2¹/₂ inches wide.

Dust the inside of an embossing pattern mould lightly with icing sugar and flick away the excess with a soft paintbrush. Press a circle of sugarpaste into the mould, pressing around the pattern, then lift it out carefully and drape the paste over a cupcake. Press in position, being careful not to touch the design. Repeat with the rest of the pink sugarpaste and five cupcakes. Using the white sugarpaste, repeat with the remaining six cakes. To finish, stick the daisies in position with a small dab of royal icing.

Baby's First Birthday Cake

Serves 25–30

For the cake base:

1 x 20 cm/8 inch, round
Madeira cake
(see page 28)
1 x 15 cm/6 inch, round
Madeira cake

To decorate:

1¹/₂ batches vanilla buttercream
1.3 kg/3 lb ready-to roll
sugarpaste
icing sugar, for dusting
pink, grey and lilac paste food
colourings
thin lilac net ribbon trim

Cut the tops of both cakes level if they have peaked, then cut each cake in half and spread one half with a little buttercream. Sandwich the cakes back together, then spread the remaining buttercream thinly over the top and sides of the cakes. Place the smaller cake on a thin, 15 cm/6 inch, round cake board.

Roll out 700 g/1¹/₂ lb sugarpaste on a surface dusted with icing sugar to a circle large enough to cover the top and sides of the 20 cm/8 inch cake. Using both hands, carefully lift over the cake and smooth down. Trim the edges and place on a cake board or flat plate. Repeat with the 15 cm/6 inch cake, using 450 g/1 lb sugarpaste to cover, then stack the small cake on top of the larger one.

Colour the scraps and 225 g/8 oz sugarpaste in three batches: pale pink, grey and lilac. Roll out thinly on a surface dusted with icing sugar and cut wide and narrow strips in all three colours, then trim and stick to the sides of the larger cake with a little cold boiled water.

Cut out small and large discs in all colours using a small round cutter or a clean bottle cap, then press on to decorate the top cake as shown. Mould scraps of grey icing into a sausage and mould into a twist for the centre of the cake as shown. Tie the lilac net ribbon around the centre of the two cakes and make a neat bow to finish.

Number 1 Birthday Cake

Serves 18–20

For the cake base:

1 x 25 cm x 20 cm/10 x 8 inch, oblong Madeira sponge cake (mixture for a 23 cm/9 inch square, see page 28)

To decorate:

2 batches vanilla buttercream
750 g/1 lb 10 oz ready-to-roll sugarpaste
yellow, red, blue and green paste food colouring
icing sugar, for dusting
assorted sweets, to decorate (optional)

Trim the top of the cake flat if it has peaked and cut away a corner and the edges to make the shape of the number 1 as shown. Cover with a quarter of the buttercream and place the cake on a large flat board or tray.

Colour two thirds of the sugarpaste yellow, roll into a thick sausage shape, flatten, then roll out on a surface dusted with icing sugar. Cut long strips, slightly deeper than the sides of the cake, with enough to go all the way around. Press the strips onto the sides of the cake, overlapping slightly onto the top and hiding any joins in the corners where they are less visible.

Roll out the remaining white sugarpaste and roughly cut out a number 1 the same size as your cake. Lift this onto the cake, ease into place, smooth down and trim the edges where it meets the yellow.

Colour half the remaining buttercream red and the rest blue. Place in piping bags with a star nozzle and pipe shells around the top and base of the cake.

Add various colours to the sugarpaste trimmings, then roll into small balls, flatten and stick on the top of the cake with a little cold boiled water. Alternatively, scatter with a few brightly coloured sweets.

It's A Gift Birthday Cake

Serves 16

For the cake base:

mixture for a 20 cm/8 inch, round
Madeira cake (*see* page 28)
baked in an oval cake tin, about
24 x 17 cm/9¹/₂ x 6¹/₂ inches
6 tbsp apricot glaze

To decorate:

1.3 kg/2³/₄ lb ready-to-roll
sugarpaste
icing sugar, for dusting
red, dark blue, bright blue, green,
pink and yellow paste
food colourings
confectioner's glaze (optional)

Trim the top of the cake if it has peaked, then brush the apricot glaze over the top and sides. Roll out 900 g/2 lb of the sugarpaste on a board dusted with icing sugar to an oval large enough to cover the top and sides of the cake. Use to cover the cake (*see* page 62), trim, then transfer to a cake board or plate. Roll out the trimmings thinly on a board dusted with icing sugar. Cut out eight blossoms using a medium-size 5-petal flower cutter.

Divide the remaining sugarpaste in half. Colour one half red, roll out, then cut out two 2.5 cm/1 inch-wide strips, one 42 cm/17 inches long, the other 38 cm/15 inches long. Brush the undersides lightly with cold boiled water and position as shown, across the cake. Trim the ends level with the bottom of the cake. Cut out two more strips 7.5 cm/3 inches long, then cut a 'V' shape in one end of each. Dampen the top and bottom of each and press on as shown, twisting them slightly. Cut two more strips, 23 cm/9 inches long, and loop each in half for the bow. Dampen and press into place.
Finally, cut a small strip, 2 cm/³/₄ inch long, dampen and press in the centre.

Divide the remaining sugarpaste into five equal pieces and colour them dark blue, bright blue, green, pink and yellow. Dampen the blossoms and press onto the cake. Shape eight tiny pieces of green and dark blue sugarpaste into circles, dampen and press into the centres of the blossoms. Roll small balls from the coloured sugarpastes, dampen and press around the bottom edge. Brush with confectioner's glaze to make them shine, if liked.

Birthday Bunting Cupcakes

Makes 12

For the cakes:

1 batch vanilla cupcakes
(*see* page 33)

To decorate:

500 g/1 lb 1 oz sugarpaste
deep pink and pale pink paste
food colourings
icing sugar, for dusting
1/4 batch white royal icing
(*see* page 50)
1/2 batch vanilla buttercream
pink sugarcraft icing pen
(optional)
24 tiny and 6 slightly larger pink
sugarpaste flowers

Trim the tops of the cupcakes if they have peaked. Reserve 50 g/2 oz of the sugarpaste. Divide the rest in half and colour one half deep pink. Roll out the deep pink and white sugarpastes separately on a board dusted with icing sugar. Stamp out three circles from each colour to fit the tops of your cakes (about 6 cm/2 1/2 inches across usually). Press the circles on top of six of the cupcakes, fixing them in place with a little white decorating icing. Spoon the buttercream into a piping bag fitted with a star nozzle and pipe a swirl over the top of the six remaining cupcakes.

Colour the reserved sugarpaste pale pink. Roll out the three colours of sugarpastes separately and cut out 18 tiny triangles to make bunting, and six rectangles the same width as the top of the cupcakes and 1 cm/1/2 inch wide. Fix three bunting triangles to the top of each sugarpaste-covered cupcake with royal icing, with tiny sugarpaste flowers in between. Decorate some of the triangles with tiny piped dots or stripes in decorating icing, piped on using a small piping bag fitted with a fine writing nozzle. Press a pattern round the edges of others with a cocktail stick.

Mark a pattern around the edges of the rectangles using a cocktail stick and press an appropriate message in the centre of each using an embossing tool, or write the message on with a pink sugarcraft pen. Attach a larger sugarpaste flower in a corner of each rectangle with decorating icing. Press a rectangle on top of each buttercream-covered cupcake.

Sixth Birthday Cake

Serves 18–20

For the cake base:

1 x 20 cm/8 inch round chocolate
sponge cake (*see* page 27)
baked in two sandwich tins
1 x 15 cm/6 inch square chocolate
sponge cake, but using half the
ingredient amounts, to give a
shallow cake (*see* page 27)

To decorate:

2¹/₂ batches chocolate buttercream
blue and green sugar-coated
chocolate beans
150 g/5 oz ready-to-roll sugarpaste
yellow and red paste food colourings
heart-shaped jelly sweets

Decorator's Tip:

Alternatively, use melted chocolate
instead of buttercream to cover
the cake (*see* page 67).

Cut the square cake in half to get two rectangles and stack one half on top of the other. Check that it is the same height as the two round sponges stacked up and, if not, trim whichever cakes are too deep until they match.

Cut one corner of the stacked square cake halves at an angle and push against the round cake to check it's a good fit, then unstack the cakes. Using a cup or can as a guide, cut a hole in the centre of one of the round cakes.

Sandwich the pairs of cakes together with a quarter of the buttercream and place on a foil-covered board or tray, joining the stem of the 6 to the round cake with buttercream. Cover the whole cake with the remaining buttercream, filling any holes, then drop the chocolate beans in the centre of the 6.

Colour half the sugarpaste yellow and the rest red, then roll into balls of two different sizes. Press them into flat discs the place on top of the cake as shown. Lean the jelly hearts around the sides of the cake, pressing in slightly. You can decorate this cake with any of your favourite sweets and add candles as part of the design, if wished.

Bright Spot Birthday Cupcakes

Makes 12

150 g/5 oz butter, softened
150 g/5 oz caster sugar
175 g/6 oz self-raising flour
3 medium eggs
1 tsp vanilla extract
2 tbsp milk

To decorate:

1 batch cream cheese frosting
(*see* page 44)
125 g/4 oz ready-to-roll sugarpaste
paste food colourings

Preheat the oven to 180˚C/350˚F/Gas Mark 4. Line a 12-hole tray with paper cases.

Place the butter and sugar in a bowl, then sift in the flour. In another bowl, beat the eggs with the vanilla extract and milk, then add to the flour mixture and beat until smooth. Spoon into the cases, filling them three-quarters full.

Bake for about 18 minutes until firm to the touch in the centre. Turn out to cool on a wire rack.

To decorate the cupcakes, swirl the top of each cupcake with a little cream cheese frosting using a small palette knife. Divide the sugarpaste into batches and colour each one separately with paste food colouring. Dust a clean, flat surface with icing sugar. Roll out the coloured icing and stamp out small coloured circles with the flat end of an icing nozzle. Press the dots onto the frosting. Keep for 3 days in a cool place in an airtight container.

Polka Dot Present Cake

Serves 12

For the cake base:

1 x 18 cm/7 inch square, all-in-one
quick-mix sponge cake
(see page 30)
5 tbsp apricot glaze

To decorate:

1.3 kg/2³/₄ lb ready-to-roll sugarpaste
icing sugar, for dusting
yellow, green, pink, blue, orange
and lavender paste food colourings
¹/₂ batch vanilla buttercream

Trim the top of the cake if it has peaked, then brush the apricot glaze over the top and sides. Roll out 900 g/2 lb of the sugarpaste on a board dusted with icing sugar to a square large enough to cover the top and sides of the cake. Use to cover the cake (see page 62), trim, then transfer the cake to a cake board or plate.

Gather up the trimmings and knead into a ball with the remaining sugarpaste. Divide in half and colour half bright yellow. Roll out the yellow sugarpaste and cut out two strips, 2 cm/³/₄ inch wide and 33 cm/13 inches long. Brush the undersides of the strips lightly with cold boiled water and position them across the middle and down the sides of the cake, crossing them in the centre. Trim the ends level with the bottom of the cake. Cut out two more strips, 10 cm/4 inches long, then cut a 'V' shape in one end of each. Dampen the top and bottom of each and press onto the cake as the ends of the ribbon bow, lifting them so they do not sit flat on the cake. Cut out two more strips, 18 cm/7 inches long, and loop each in half to form the bow. Dampen the ends and press into place. Cut one small strip, 2 cm/³/₄ inch long, dampen and press in the centre of the bow, tucking the ends under.

Divide the remaining sugarpaste into five equal pieces and colour them green, pink, blue, orange and lavender. Roll out each and cut out 1 cm/¹/₂ inch circles – you will need about 65. Dampen the circles and press over the top and sides of the cake. Colour the buttercream dark blue and spoon into a piping bag fitted with a star nozzle. Pipe a border of shells around the base of the cake to finish.

Bright Birthday Cupcakes

Makes 16

For the cakes:

1½ batches vanilla cupcakes
(see page 33)

To decorate:

1 batch cream cheese frosting
(see page 44)
1 batch vanilla buttercream
dark pink, turquoise, bright red,
purple, green, orange and pale
yellow paste food colourings
2 dark pink sugarpaste flowers
2 large dark pink sugar pearls
1 tbsp blue or lavender crystal
sugar sprinkles
1 tbsp green sugar strands
50 g/2 oz ready-to-roll sugarpaste
½ tbsp tiny white sugar sprinkles
½ tbsp tiny red sugar sprinkles
14 coloured sugar-coated chocolate
sweets

Trim the tops of the cakes if they have peaked. Divide the cream cheese frosting into thirds and colour one third dark pink, one turquoise and one bright red. Divide the buttercream into fifths, colouring one fifth purple, one green, and one orange and leave the rest plain. Using a large piping bag fitted with a plain nozzle, pipe a **pink** swirl on top of two cupcakes, starting at the outside and working towards the centre. Top both with a sugarpaste flower and fix a sugar pearl in the centre of each with a dab of buttercream. Spread **purple** buttercream over the top of two cupcakes with a palette knife. Sprinkle over the crystal sugar. Using a large piping bag fitted with a star nozzle and holding the bag upright, start in the middle of a cupcake and pipe a tight **turquoise** swirl in the centre. Continue piping in a spiral, lowering the bag to an angle of 60 degrees to the top of the cake until you reach the outside edge. Repeat. Spread **green** buttercream over the top of two cupcakes with a palette knife. Put the sugar strands in a shallow dish and dip in each cupcake to cover. Using a palette knife, spread the tops of two cupcakes with plain buttercream. Colour the sugarpaste pale **yellow**, then pull off tiny-pea-size pieces and press into thin, flat circles. Spread out on a plate and prick faces in each with a pin. Gently press over the buttercream. Using a piping bag fitted with a small star nozzle, pipe small **orange** stars over the tops of two cupcakes, holding the bag upright. Scatter tiny white sugar sprinkles over. Using three quarters of the **red** cream cheese frosting in a piping bag fitted with a large plain nozzle, pipe a swirl on the top of two cupcakes, starting at the outside and working towards the centre. Then, using a small plain nozzle, pipe a swirl in the centre of each cake, starting in the middle, to create a small spiral in the centre of each. Scatter with red sugar sprinkles. Using the rest of the buttercream in a piping bag fitted with a star nozzle, pipe a swirl on the last two cupcakes. Arrange sugar-coated **sweets** in different colours on top of each to finish.

Toy Bricks Birthday Cake

Serves 10–12

For the cakes:

2 x 20 cm/8 inch square Madeira
cakes (*see* page 30)

To decorate:

150 g/5 oz ready-to-roll sugarpaste
red, yellow, blue and green paste
food colourings
icing sugar, for dusting
3 batches cream cheese frosting
(*see* page 44)
1/2 batch royal icing (*see* page 50)

Decorator's Tip:

Instead of using sugarpaste
to make the coloured cutout
decorations, these can be made
with flooded royal icing, left to dry
on waxed paper, then stuck
onto the sides of the cake.

Divide the sugarpaste into four portions and colour one red, one
yellow, one blue and one green. Either roll these pieces out on a
board or surface dusted with icing sugar and use cutters, or just
model 20 shapes to decorate the sides of the cakes, adding
details with thinly rolled pieces of various colours. Leave to dry.

Trim the tops of the cakes level and trim off all the crusts. Place
one on top of the other. Measure the cakes – you need the height
of the pile to be half the length of one side, so take them apart
and trim again if you need to. Finally, sandwich them together
with a little cream cheese frosting and cut across the top of the
cake each way to make four cubes. Wrap them in foil and chill in
the freezer (*see* page 26).

Cover each cube of cake carefully with the cream cheese
frosting, making them as smooth as you can, then press the
sugarpaste decorations onto the tops and sides.

Divide the royal icing into four portions and colour one red, one
yellow, one blue and one green. Place each in a paper piping
bag and pipe lines around all the edges of the cakes, adding
details to the decorations. Carefully lift each brick onto a plate
and touch up any piping that may have fallen off before serving.

Blue Ribbon Gift Cake

Serves 20

For the cake base:

1 x 20 cm/8 inch square Madeira cake (*see* page 28)

To decorate:

^{1}/$_2$ batch vanilla buttercream
1.25 kg/2^1/$_2$ lb ready-to-roll sugarpaste
icing sugar, for dusting
turquoise, pale blue, yellow and pink paste food colourings

Trim the top of the cake if it has peaked and cut the cake in half horizontally. Spread the buttercream over one half, then sandwich the layers back together. Spread the top and sides of the cake with the remaining buttercream.

Roll out 700 g/1^1/$_2$ lb sugarpaste on a surface dusted with icing sugar to a square large enough to cover the top and sides of the cake. Lift the sugarpaste onto the cake and smooth down over the top and sides. Trim the edges neatly, then place on a cake board. Reroll the sugarpaste thinly and cut out 16 large white daisy shapes with a daisy cutter.

Colour two thirds of the remaining sugarpaste turquoise and roll out to a long, thin strip. Cut out three ribbon strips, 36 cm/14 inches long by 4 cm/1^1/$_2$ inches wide. Lightly brush the underside of each ribbon with cold boiled water, then stick two ribbons over the cake as shown. Using the remaining ribbon, form two loops with short pieces together to make a bow, then trail two strips over the cake, cutting a 'V' shape in the end of each. Neaten the join in the centre with a scrap of sugarpaste.

Brush the underside of each daisy with a little cold boiled water and stick the daisies onto the top and sides of the cake. Colour scraps of white sugarpaste blue, yellow and pink and roll into small balls. Dampen each ball lightly and press into the centre of each daisy to finish.

Cute Creatures Easter Cupcakes

Makes 12

For the cakes:

1 batch vanilla cupcakes
(*see* page 33)

To decorate:

450 g/1 lb ready-to-roll sugarpaste
pink, orange, blue, yellow, green
and mauve paste food colourings
icing sugar, for dusting
1 batch vanilla buttercream
tiny edible metallic balls
2 tbsp royal icing (*see* page 50), or
a small tube of royal icing

Colour 25 g/1 oz sugarpaste deep pink, 50 g/2 oz light pink, 25 g/1 oz orange, 50 g/2 oz blue, 50 g/2 oz yellow, 25 g/1 oz green and 25 g/1 oz mauve and leave the remainder white. Roll out the deep pink paste on a board or surface dusted with icing sugar and cut out 12 daisies using a medium daisy stamp. Repeat with the white sugarpaste, using a larger daisy and stamp out 12 white daisies. Roll the orange sugarpaste into 24 small carrot shapes. Mould the light pink sugarpaste into four pink rabbits and repeat with the blue sugarpaste, making four blue rabbits. Model the yellow sugarpaste into four chicks. Roll scraps into small ovals for tiny eggs and make coloured centres for the daisies from scraps. Leave all the pieces to dry for 1 hour on nonstick baking parchment.

Trim the tops of the cakes flat if they have peaked. Colour the buttercream pale green and place in a piping bag fitted with a star nozzle. Pipe a thick swirl onto the top of each cupcake, then arrange a pink and white daisy and two carrots on each cake. Make carrot tops from small green strips of sugarpaste. Place the chicks on four cakes and repeat with the blue and pink rabbits. Make beaks for the chicks. Press metallic balls on the animals for eyes and decorate the rabbits' faces with royal icing as shown. Arrange the eggs on the cakes in batches of three to finish.

Baby Chick Easter Cake

Serves 24

For the cake base:

1 x all-in-one quick-mix cake
baked in a 900 ml/1¹/₂ pint
pudding basin (*see* page 30)
1 x all-in-one quick-mix cake
baked in a 1 litre/2 pint
pudding basin
1 x all-in-one quick-mix cake baked
in 2 x 20 cm/8 inch sandwich tins

To decorate:

1¹/₂ batches vanilla buttercream
1.5 kg/3¹/₄ lb ready-to-roll
sugarpaste
green, yellow, orange, pink, blue
and black paste food colourings
icing sugar, for dusting
bought butterfly and ladybird
iced decorations

Cut a slice from the dome of the large cake, turn it over. Trim both cakes flat if peaked. Sandwich the two trimmed sides of the cakes together with buttercream. Trim to a smooth shape. Sandwich the round sponges together with buttercream, then spread buttercream over the top and sides and place on a cake board. Spread the chick shape all over with buttercream.

Colour 575 g/1¹/₄ lb sugarpaste green and use to cover the top and sides of the round cake (*see* page 62). Press the edges to spread out onto the board. Colour 450 g/1 lb sugarpaste yellow, 225 g/8 oz orange, 175 g/6 oz pink and 50 g/2 oz blue. Roll out the yellow to a thin circle and use to cover the chick. Cut out small wings. Roll out the pink thinly to an oblong and press on a fancy pattern with an embossing tool. Make a smaller strip for the bow. Dampen the large strip with cold boiled water, stick to the base of the chick and place the bow on its head. Roll out the white to a small circle and cut into sharp points. Dampen and stick to the base of the chick for the eggshell. Mould the orange into a beak, hair and feet, then stick on. Roll out the blue into two small discs for eyes and a circle and thin sausage for a dummy. Attach the eyes to the chick and press on small white balls of sugarpaste. Paint features on the eyes with black paste colouring. Roll out a thin white strip of sugarpaste, drape it round the chick and attach the dummy to this. Model a pink teat for the dummy and stick on. Press green sugarpaste through a garlic press to make grass and place on the green cake. Make leaves with the scraps. Press out large daisies with a flower stamp from yellow and pink scraps, making balls for the centres, then decorate the sides of the cake with the butterflies and ladybirds. Place the chick onto the green cake to finish.

Summer Sunflower Cupcakes

Makes 18

For the cakes:

150 g/5 oz butter, softened
150 g/5 oz caster sugar
3 medium eggs, beaten
150 g/5 oz self-raising flour
½ tsp baking powder
1 small orange

To decorate:

1 batch buttercream (*see* page 42)
yellow and orange food colourings

Preheat the oven to 180°C/350°F/Gas Mark 4 and line two bun trays with 18 paper fairy-cake cases.

Place the butter, sugar and beaten eggs in a bowl, then sift in the flour and baking powder. Finely grate the zest from the orange into the bowl and squeeze out 2 tablespoons juice.

Beat together for about 2 minutes, preferably with an electric hand–mixer, until pale and fluffy. Spoon the mixture into the paper cases and bake for about 15 minutes until firm and golden. Cool on a wire rack.

To decorate, colour three quarters of the buttercream bright yellow and the remainder orange. Place in two piping bags fitted with star nozzles. Pipe a border of straight lines round the outer edges to form petals. Pipe more petals to fill in the centres. Pipe a circle of orange dots in the centre of each to finish. Keep for 3 days in a cool place.

Halloween Mice Cake

Serves 10–12

For the cake base:

1 batch 20 cm/8 inch, round rich
chocolate cake mix (*see* page
27) baked in 2 x 1.1 litre/2 pint
heatproof basins for 40 minutes,
or until a skewer pressed into
the centre of each cake comes
out clean

To decorate:

1 batch chocolate buttercream
700 g/1½ lb ready-to-roll
sugarpaste
orange, green and brown paste
food colourings
icing sugar, for dusting
black sugarcraft icing pen

Trim the tops of the cakes level if they have peaked and sandwich them together with some of the buttercream to make a ball. Spread the remaining buttercream over the outside of the cake.

Colour 400 g/14 oz sugarpaste orange and use to cover the cake (*see* page 62). Mark ridges down the sides with the handle of a wooden spoon to give a realistic pumpkin shape. Colour half the remaining sugarpaste green and shape a stalk. Dampen the base of this and press on top of the cake. Roll out small pieces of the paste and cut out two leaves with a sharp knife or leaf cutter. Mark veins on the leaves with a knife, dampen them and press onto the lower part of the cake at the front and the back. Roll two long, thin, green sausages, dampen and press onto the front and back of the cake, looping as shown, from the stalk to the leaves.

Cut two holes in the sugarpaste either side of the stalk, for the mice's heads to poke out, and holes beneath for their tails. Reserve a very tiny piece of white sugarpaste to make eyes for the mice and colour the rest light brown. Shape the heads of the mice and press two tiny white eyes on each. Push a cocktail stick into each of the higher holes in the cake and press a mouse head onto it. Shape ears and feet out of the remaining brown sugarpaste, then dampen and press into place. Mark smiling mouths with the point of a sharp knife and draw pupils onto the eyes with a black sugarcraft pen. Add a small orange sugarpaste nose to one mouse, fixing it in place with a dab of cold boiled water. Shape two tails from brown sugarpaste, dampen and press on as shown.

Witch's Hat Halloween Cake

Serves 8–10

For the cake base:

1 x 15 cm/6 inch, round chocolate
cake (*see* page 27)
4 tbsp apricot glaze

To decorate:

900 g/2 lb ready-to-roll sugarpaste
purple, green, brown, black and
orange paste food colourings
icing sugar, for dusting
thin cake board
1 tube black royal decorating icing
thin gold ribbon trim (optional)

Trim the top of the cake if it has peaked, then brush the apricot glaze over the top and sides of the cake. Colour 600 g/1 lb 5 oz sugarpaste purple and use to cover the cake (*see* page 62). Trim, reserving the trimmings. Brush a thin cake board measuring about 25.5 cm/10 inches with water. Colour 150 g/5 oz sugarpaste green, roll it out very thinly and use to cover the cake board. Reserve the trimmings. Lift the cake onto the board.

Divide the rest of the sugarpaste in half, reserving a small white piece and a tiny piece to colour brown, and colour one half black and the other orange. Roll a thin sausage of orange sugarpaste, about 35.5 cm/14 inches long, dampen and press around the base of the cake. Flatten and mark a pattern on it using the blade of a small knife. Model a pointed witch's hat and a cauldron from black sugarpaste. Roll tiny balls of green sugarpaste and press them into the top of the cauldron. Cut out about 12 tiny stars from a little purple sugarpaste, dampen and press over the hat. Roll a thin sausage of orange sugarpaste, dampen and press around the base of the hat. Dampen the bottom of the hat and position on the cake. Mould four small pumpkins out of orange sugarpaste, mark indentations around the sides with a cocktail stick and shape leaves and stalks from the green and brown sugarpastes. Dampen and press into place on top.

Using black decorating icing, pipe a spider's web around the top of the cake and with eight threads coming halfway down the sides. Roll eight small balls of black sugarpaste, flatten them into ovals and dampen. Press them around the sides, on the threads, for the spiders' bodies. Add black sugarpaste legs and white sugarpaste eyes with tiny black sugarpaste pupils. Position the pumpkins. Trim the board with thin ribbon, if wished.

Smiling Pumpkin Cake

Serves 10–12

For the cake base:

1 batch 13 cm/5 inch square
Madeira cake mixture baked in a
2 litre/4 pint bowl (*see* page 28)
4 tbsp apricot glaze

To decorate:

1.1 kg/2½ lb ready-to-roll
sugarpaste
orange, green and black paste
food colourings
icing sugar, for dusting

Trim the top of the cake level if it has peaked, then brush the apricot glaze over the domed side of the cake.

Colour 900 g/2 lb sugarpaste orange, roll it out on a board dusted with icing sugar to a round large enough to cover the cake. Using both hands, carefully lift it over the cake and smooth down. Trim the bottom edge level.

Colour half the remaining sugarpaste green and shape it into a stalk to sit on top of the pumpkin. Colour the rest of the sugarpaste black.

Roll six very thin sausages of black sugarpaste long enough to fit over the cake. Brush the sausages with a little cold boiled water and position them at regular intervals over the cake. Press them gently into place and trim the bottom edges neatly.

Roll out the rest of the black sugarpaste, and cut out three small triangles for eyes and a nose. Cut out a wide, smiley mouth (perhaps with a tooth missing!) that will stretch between two of the black sausages. Dampen the triangles and the pumpkin mouth and gently press into place. Finally, dampen the underside of the stalk and press this on top of the cake.

Starbright Fireworks Cupcakes

Makes 12

125 g/4 oz butter, softened
125 g/4 oz caster sugar
125 g/4 oz self-raising flour
2 medium eggs
1 tsp vanilla extract

To decorate

icing sugar, for dusting
225 g/8 oz ready-to-roll sugarpaste
dust or paste food colourings
1 batch cream cheese frosting
(*see* page 44)
edible silver balls (optional)
small candles

Preheat the oven to 180°C/350°F/Gas Mark 4. Line a 12-hole tray with deep paper cases.

Place the butter and sugar in a bowl, then sift in the flour. In another bowl, beat the eggs with the vanilla extract, then add to the flour mixture. Beat until smooth, then spoon into the cases, filling them three-quarters full.

Bake for about 18 minutes until firm to the touch in the centre. Turn out to cool on a wire rack.

To decorate the cupcakes, dust a clean, flat surface with icing sugar. Colour the sugarpaste in batches of bright colours, such as blue, yellow and orange. Roll each out thinly and cut out stars with a cutter or follow the pattern on page 253. Leave to dry out for 2 hours until firm. Place the frosting in a piping bag fitted with a star nozzle and pipe large swirls on top of each cupcake. Decorate each cupcake with stars, edible silver balls, if using, and small candles. Keep for 2 days in an airtight container in a cool place.

Snowman Cake

Serves 16–20

For the cake:

1 x 23 cm/9 inch, round
all-in-one quick-mix sponge cake
(*see* page 30)
1 x 15 cm/6 inch square, all-in-one
quick-mix sponge cake

To decorate:

1 batch royal icing (*see* page 50)
blue, red, black and green paste
food colourings
2¹/₂ batches vanilla buttercream
large round cardboard, measuring
about 51 cm/20 inches in diameter

Trim the top of the round cake with a sharp knife into a rounded shape for the snowman's body. Carve the sides to shape the arms and the bottom of the body. Trim the top of the square cake to a rounded shape for the snowman's head and carve two thirds of the sides to shape his round face and the last third for the hat, leaving the top straight.

Colour three quarters of the royal icing blue and spread over the top three quarters of the board. Spread white royal icing over the bottom quarter (reserving a little), roughing it up a little with a round-bladed knife to resemble snow. Before the icing has set, position the body and head on the board, pressing both into the royal icing. Leave until the icing has set, then spoon the reserved white royal icing into a piping bag fitted with a small star nozzle and pipe tiny 'snowflakes' over the blue icing. Leave to set.

Reserve 1¹/₂ batches of the buttercream, divide the rest equally between three bowls and colour one red, one black and one green. Spoon the coloured buttercreams into large piping bags, each fitted with a star nozzle, and pipe stars and lines over the cakes using the three colours for the hat, scarf, buttons, eyes and mouth of the snowman. You can follow the design in the picture or create your own patterns if you prefer. Pipe or spoon a flat circle of red buttercream for the nose. Spoon the reserved vanilla buttercream into a large piping bag fitted with a star nozzle and pipe stars over the rest of the snowman to cover him completely, working around what you have already piped, taking care not to smudge or pipe over your work.

Snowmen Cupcakes

Makes 12

For the cakes:

2 egg whites
125 g/4 oz caster sugar
1 batch vanilla cupcakes
(*see* page 33)

To decorate:

450 g/1 lb ready-to-roll sugarpaste
orange, pink, blue and green paste
food colourings
1 batch vanilla buttercream
125 g/4 oz shredded soft coconut
small and large chocolate chips

Preheat the oven to 140°C/275°F/Gas Mark 1. Place the egg whites in a clean, dry bowl and whisk with an electric mixer until stiff. Whisk in the caster sugar gradually, whisking constantly, until stiff glossy peaks form. Spoon the meringue into a large piping bag fitted with a large plain nozzle. On a baking sheet lined with nonstick baking parchment, pipe 12 circles about 6 cm/2¹/₂ inches across. Pipe a small ball on top of each one to make a snowman shape and bake for about 45 minutes until pale and crisp. Leave to cool on a wire rack.

Colour the sugarpaste in four batches, one orange, one pink, one blue and one green. Trim the tops of the cakes flat if they have peaked.

Spread a little buttercream on top of each cake, then stick a meringue snowman firmly on top. Spread each snowman all over with buttercream, then press the shredded coconut onto this. Repeat with the remaining cakes.

Model the coloured sugarpastes into hats and scarves and mark indentations onto the scarves with a pasta wheel to represent knitting. Place the hats and scarves onto the snowmen. Make carrot noses out of orange scraps and place on the faces. Make eyes with the larger chocolate chips and use the smaller ones to make a mouth.

Animals

From the tiny bumblebee to the giant elephant, animals make a fun and bright theme for children's cakes and cupcakes. Roll out some sugarpaste and get inspired by these exciting projects. If you've got a cheeky monkey in your midst, the Monkey Island Cake is bound to go down a treat, whilst young horse lovers will be delighted by the Ponies in their Stable Cake.

Fuzzy Bear Cake

Serves 30

For the cake base:

1 x all-in-one quick-mix sponge
baked in a 900 ml/1½ pint
pudding basin (*see* page 32)
1 x all-in-one quick-mix sponge
baked in a 1.1 litre/2 pint
pudding basin
1 x all-in-one quick-mix sponge
baked in an 18 cm/7 inch
round cake tin

To decorate:

chocolate mint stick sweets
2 batches vanilla buttercream
brown paste food colouring
2 chocolate bean sweets
1 soft prune
candles

Cut the top of the larger cake flat and place upside down on a cake board with the dome shape uppermost. Cut a thin slice from one side of the smaller cake. Cut the smaller round cake into ears, arms and legs as shown in the diagram on page 245. Assemble the pieces as shown in the diagram using chocolate stick sweets to secure the pieces to each other.

Colour the buttercream light brown and use a little to stick the pieces of the bear together. Place the remaining buttercream in a large piping bag fitted with a star nozzle and pipe stars all over the bear, making sure to cover the whole cake. Press 2 chocolate beans into the face for eyes and a prune for his nose, then arrange candles in front of the bear to finish.

Happy Pig Cupcakes

Makes 12

For the cake base:

1 batch chocolate cupcakes
(*see* page 33)

To decorate:

1¹/₂ batches vanilla buttercream
green, brown and pink paste
food colourings
200 g/7 oz ready-to-roll sugarpaste
small amount of royal icing (optional)

Trim the tops of the cupcakes if they have peaked. Colour two thirds of the buttercream green and spoon into a large piping bag fitted with a medium plain nozzle. Pipe random lines and swirls backwards and forwards over the cupcakes to cover the tops right to the edge.

Colour the remaining buttercream dark brown and spoon into a piping bag fitted with a large plain nozzle. Pipe a wide swirl in the centre of each cupcake, leaving half the green buttercream visible. Gently rough up the brown buttercream with a knife, hollowing out the centre a little, without disturbing the green buttercream swirls.

Cut off a tiny piece of the sugarpaste and colour this dark brown to make the pigs' features. Colour the remainder pink. For the pigs, shape the pink sugarpaste into 12 circles, about 3 cm/1¹/₄ inches in diameter. Roll 12 small pieces of pink sugarpaste into balls, flatten, dampen and press into place for the pigs' snouts. Shape 24 ears from the remaining pink sugarpaste, dampen and press two onto each pig's head.

Roll tiny pieces of dark brown sugarpaste into 24 circles, dampen and press two on each pig's head for eyes. Shape 24 tiny sausages from dark brown sugarpaste, flatten, dampen and press two on each pig's snout for nostrils. Alternatively, use piped brown royal icing for these features. Carefully position a pig in the centre of each cupcake, pressing down gently into the brown buttercream.

Teddies' Party Cake

Serves 10–12

For the cake base:

1 x 20 cm/8 inch Madeira cake
(*see* page 28)
6 tbsp apricot glaze

To decorate:

575 g/1¼ lb white marzipan
green, brown, pink, yellow, red
and black paste food colourings
cake varnishing gloss (optional)
350 kg/12 oz ready-to-roll
sugarpaste
icing sugar, for dusting
red royal icing tube
edible gold balls

Cut the top of the cake level and brush the cake with apricot glaze. Colour the marzipan light green and use to cover the cake (*see* page 62). Flute the base up, pinching between your thumb and forefinger. Brush on cake varnishing gloss, if liked, to give a shiny finish.

Roll out 125 g/4 oz sugarpaste thinly on a surface dusted with icing sugar and use to cover a 25 cm/10 inch cake board. Trim the edges then place the cake onto the covered board.

Colour 250 g/9 oz sugarpaste light brown, 25 g/1 oz pink, 25 g/1 oz yellow, 25 g/1 oz red and 25 g/1 oz black. Model the light brown sugarpaste into two bears and make pink faces and paws. Roll small black balls and press on for noses. Make white balls with small black dots for eyes.

Arrange one bear to be 'climbing' onto the cake and sit the other on top. Mould a brown barrel with scraps and mark with a skewer. Roll out white sugarpaste thinly, cut into a strip and position slightly 'ruffled' as shown.

Roll out the pink and white sugarpastes and stamp into daisies and circles. Stick to the sides of the cake, then roll small yellow balls for daisy centres and press onto the flowers. Mould the red sugarpaste into small cups and make tongues for the bears. Write your message on the white strip with red royal icing. Sprinkle the top of the cake with gold balls to finish.

Farmyard Carousel Cake

Serves 12–14

For the cake base:

1 x 20 cm/8 inch, round Madeira
cake (see page 28)
1 x 20 cm/8 inch, all-in-one quick-
mix sandwich layer (see page 30)

To decorate:

strong glue
1 piece 20 cm/8 inch long thick
wooden dowelling
white paper
thin red ribbon trim
1/2 batch vanilla buttercream
1.75 kg/3 1/2 lb ready-to-roll
sugarpaste
green, blue, brown, yellow, red,
grey, pink and orange
paste food colourings
icing sugar, for dusting

Using strong glue, stick a 20 cm/8 inch thin cake board onto the length of thick wooden dowelling and leave until firmly set. Glue a strip of white paper round the dowelling, then stick round a piece of thin red ribbon. Cut the top of the large cake completely flat, spread the top and sides with buttercream and place on a thin, 30 cm/12 inch, round cake board. Trim the sandwich cake to give a sloping effect and coat with buttercream. Colour 700 g/1 1/2 lb sugarpaste green, 125 g/4 oz blue, 125 g/4 oz brown, 350 g/12 oz yellow, 125 g/4 oz red, 25 g/1 oz grey, 50 g/2 oz pink and 25 g/1 oz orange, leaving the rest white. Use the green sugarpaste to cover the large cake (see page 62). Use the trimmings to cover the edge of the cake board. Roll a thick blue sugarpaste strip to go round the cake, dampen lightly and stick in place. Roll the brown sugarpaste into thin strips and stick over the blue to form a fence. Mark with a knife for a wooden effect. Use green trimmings to make strands of grass and foliage as shown. Mould appropriately coloured sugarpastes into animals and use trimmings to make the details, as shown. Use scraps and a small daisy cutter to stamp out flowers; decorate as shown.

Stand the sandwich cake on the pole between two suitable supports, such as pudding basins, to hold it upright whilst decorating. Use the yellow sugarpaste to cover the cake. Cut out a yellow strip, 2 cm/3/4 inch wide, with a fluted pasta wheel. Roll out the red sugarpaste and cut out tapering strips as shown. Stick the red and yellow strips over and around the cake with a little cold boiled water. Make a red ball for the centre and stick down. Press the cake on the pole down into the green cake, making sure it is firmly wedged, and decorate the join with green trimmings. Place the animals round the cake as shown.

Kitty Faces Cupcakes

Makes 14–16

125 g/4 oz self-raising flour
125 g/4 oz caster sugar
125 g/4 oz soft margarine
2 medium eggs, beaten
1 tsp vanilla extract

To decorate:

1 batch buttercream
(*see* page 42)
pink paste food colouring
50 g/2 oz desiccated coconut
liquorice all-sorts sweets
red gel writing icing tube

Preheat the oven to 180°C/350°F/Gas Mark 4. Line two 12-hole bun trays with 12–14 paper fairy-cake cases or silicone moulds, depending on the depth of the holes.

Sift the flour into a bowl and stir together with the caster sugar. Add the margarine, eggs and vanilla extract and beat together for about 2 minutes until smooth.

Spoon into the cases and bake for 15–20 minutes until golden and firm to the touch. Turn out on a wire rack. When cool, trim the tops flat if they have peaked slightly.

Colour the buttercream pink and spread over the top of each cake. Pour the coconut onto a shallow dish. Press the top of each iced cupcake into the coconut. Cut the sweets to form pink ears, eyes, a jelly nose and whiskers and pipe on a red mouth in red gel icing. Keep in an airtight container in a cool place for 2 days.

Piggies in the Mud Cake

Serves 14–18

For the cake base:

1 x 20 cm/8 inch, round chocolate
cake (*see* page 27)

To decorate:

¹/₂ batch vanilla buttercream
450 g/1 lb ready-to-roll chocolate
sugarpaste
icing sugar, for dusting
450 g/1 lb ready-to-roll
white sugarpaste
green, pink and yellow paste
food colourings
400 g/14 oz milk chocolate, broken
into squares
28 chocolate wafer finger biscuits

Cut the cake in half, spread the bottom layer with buttercream, then sandwich the cakes back together. Spread the top and sides of the cake with buttercream. Roll out the chocolate sugarpaste on a surface dusted with icing sugar to a circle large enough to cover the top and sides of the cake. Drape the icing over, smooth down and trim the edges.

Colour 225 g/8 oz white sugarpaste light green and roll out thinly. Cover a thin cake board with the green paste, then mark with the tines of a fork to represent grass. Place the cake on the board. Colour 125 g/4 oz sugarpaste pink and model into pigs' bodies, heads and arms, and bottoms.

Melt the chocolate in a heatproof bowl standing over a pan of simmering water. Dip each chocolate wafer biscuit in the chocolate to cover, remove from the bowl and stick onto the sides of the cake. Make a rough pattern with the tines of a fork to represent wood bark while the chocolate is still wet. Repeat with the remaining biscuits. Place the pigs' bodies on top of the cake as shown. Pour the remaining melted chocolate round them to form their muddy pool.

Roll out green sugarpaste scraps to make trailing plants and leaves and stick round the sides of the pool. Roll out the remaining scraps of sugarpaste, then stamp out small coloured daisies and place on the grass. Make yellow centres for the flowers and stick in place to finish.

Ducky Duck Cake

Serves 10–12

For the cake base:

1 x all-in-one quick-mix sponge
baked in two 20 cm/8 inch
sandwich tins (*see* page 30)
1 x all-in-one quick-mix sponge
baked in a 15 cm/6 inch, round
tin (*see* page 30)

To decorate:

1½ batches vanilla buttercream
yellow and orange paste
food colourings
125 g/4 oz ready-to-roll sugarpaste
75 g/3 oz shredded soft coconut
thin chocolate mint stick sweets
2 white marshmallows
2 black fruit pastille sweets

Cut the large cake in half lengthways to form two half-moon shapes, sandwich together with a little buttercream and stand with the flat side uppermost. Cut the small cake as shown on page 244, and stick the head, back and tail together with buttercream as in the diagram.

Colour the remaining buttercream yellow and the sugarpaste orange. Spread the yellow buttercream over the duck to cover completely, flicking up occasionally with a palette knife to represent feathers. Toss the coconut in a little yellow food colouring, then press onto the buttercream.

Mould the orange sugarpaste into a beak shape. Press 4 chocolate stick sweets into the front of the duck's head, then press the beak onto these. Decorate the face; make two eyes with white marshmallows, then dab 2 black sweets with buttercream and stick onto the white marshmallows as shown to finish.

Ponies in their Stable Cake

Serves 12–14

For the cake base:

1 x 20 cm/8 inch, square Madeira
cake (*see* page 28)

To decorate:

1.2 kg/2¹/2 lb ready-to-roll
sugarpaste
black, brown, green, lilac, pink
and yellow paste food
colourings
¹/2 batch vanilla buttercream
icing sugar, for dusting
cocktail sticks

Colour 700 g/1¹/2 lb sugarpaste light grey with a little black food colouring, then colour 225 g/8 oz dark grey, 75 g/3 oz brown, 50 g/2 oz black, 25 g/1 oz green, and 15 g/¹/2 oz each lilac, pink and yellow. Reserve a tiny amount of white. Cut the top of the cake flat if it has peaked. Cut the cake in half down the middle. Spread one half with buttercream, then sandwich one half on top of the other. Spread all over with buttercream. Spread a 25 cm/10 inch cake board thinly with a little buttercream. Thinly roll out the dark grey sugarpaste on a surface dusted with icing sugar and cover the board, trim, then mark on a tiled pattern. Use the light grey sugarpaste to thinly cover the cake (*see* page 62). Place the cake on the covered board. Using a round-bladed knife, mark on a wooden effect. Cut out three 'windows' at the front. Use the black sugarpaste to fill in the spaces.

Make the ponies' heads. Roll 15 g/¹/2 oz each of black, brown and grey sugarpaste into three balls. Press the front of each ball down to elongate into a muzzle shape, then make ears from the scraps. Place each on a cocktail stick and stick into a stable window. Roll strands of contrasting sugarpaste thinly to make the manes and mark on nostrils with a skewer. Use white sugarpaste to fashion eyes and extra markings, if liked.

Roll the remaining brown sugarpaste into thin sausages and decorate the sides and roof, sticking on with a little cold boiled water. Using small cutters, make ivy leaves with the green sugarpaste and pink, yellow and lilac daisies, and decorate as shown. Press green scraps round the base of the cake and mark with a skewer for grass. Add a few small daisies to finish.

In the Jungle Cake

Serves 10–12

For the cake base:

1 x 20 cm/8 inch Madeira cake
(see page 28)

To decorate:

1 batch vanilla buttercream
green, grey, yellow,
brown, pink and black
paste food colourings
1.25 kg/2¹/₄ lb ready-to-roll
sugarpaste
icing sugar, for dusting

Colour a quarter of the buttercream green, place in a piping bag fitted with a star nozzle and reserve. Cut the top of the cake level and spread with a little buttercream, then spread the remainder over the sides.

Colour 575 g/1¹/₄ lb sugarpaste light green and use to cover the cake (see page 62). Roll out 125 g/4 oz white sugarpaste thinly and use to cover a 25 cm/10 inch cake board. Trim, then place the cake onto the covered board. Pipe a shell border round the base of the cake with the green buttercream.

Colour 125 g/4 oz sugarpaste grey, 75 g/3 oz yellow, 50 g/2 oz brown, 25 g/1 oz dark green, 15 g/¹/₂ oz pink and 50 g/2 oz black. Model the grey sugarpaste into a round for the elephant's head, then pull out into a trunk shape. Make an oval-shaped body, short arms and legs, and flat ears. Stick the pieces together with a little cold boiled water and mark details with a skewer. Model white tusks and eyes and stick onto the elephant. Model the yellow sugarpaste into a round for the giraffe's body, then pull out to make a long neck. Make legs, ears and horns as shown. Paint the giraffe with brown dots. Make a black coil and place by the side of the cake for a snake, adding white eyes and a pink tongue. Make a zebra's head from the remaining white sugarpaste. Roll black scraps into thin sausages and place on the head for stripes, then stick on a black nose and white balls for eyes. Roll the brown sugarpaste into long, thin sausages and stick to the cake. Make small green leaves and stick near to the brown vines as shown.

Pink Butterfly Cakes

Makes 12

150 g/5 oz butter,
softened at room temperature
150 g/5 oz caster sugar
3 medium eggs, beaten
1 tsp vanilla extract
150 g/5 oz self-raising flour
$\frac{1}{2}$ tsp baking powder

To decorate

225 g/8 oz ready-to-roll
sugarpaste
pink and brown paste
food colourings
1 batch cream cheese frosting
(see page 44)
gel writing icing tubes

Preheat the oven to 180°C/350°F/Gas Mark 4 and line a 12-hole tray with deep paper cases.

Place the butter, sugar, eggs and vanilla extract in a bowl and then sift in the flour and baking powder. Beat together with an electric hand-mixer for about 2 minutes until pale and fluffy. Spoon into the paper cases and bake for 20–25 minutes until firm and golden. Cool on a wire rack.

To decorate, take the sugarpaste and colour 200 g/7 oz pale pink and the remainder brown. Roll out the sugarpaste thinly and, using a cutter or freehand, cut out four petal shapes for the wings for each cupcake and set them on nonstick baking parchment or clingfilm. Cut out 48 shapes altogether and leave to dry flat until firm (about 2 hours). Colour the cream cheese frosting bright pink and place in a piping bag fitted with a star nozzle.

Swirl pink icing on top of each cupcake, then press four wings on top of each. Mould the brown icing into body shapes and place on each cupcake. Pipe dots on the wings with tubes of gel writing icing. Keep for 2 days in an airtight container in a cool place.

Under the Sea Cake

Serves 12–14

For the cake base:

1 x 20 cm/8 inch, round Madeira cake (*see* page 28)

To decorate:

1 batch vanilla buttercream
1.25 kg/2¹/₂ lb ready-to roll sugarpaste
turquoise, light blue, green, orange, pink, yellow and black paste food colourings
icing sugar, for dusting
gold lustre powder
small birthday candles

Cut the top of the cake level, then cut in half and spread one half with a little buttercream. Sandwich the cake back together. Colour 575 g/1¹/₄ lb sugarpaste turquoise, 50 g/2 oz pale blue, 225 g/8 oz lime green, 75 g/3 oz orange, 50 g/2 oz bright pink, 25 g/1 oz yellow and 25 g/1 oz black and leave the remainder white. Use the turquoise sugarpaste to thinly cover the cake (*see* page 62). Roll 125 g/4 oz white sugarpaste into a thin sausage and press round the base of the cake. Mark on shell shapes with a clean, small, ridged bottle cap. Roll out a thin strip of white sugarpaste and place across the front of the cake.

Roll 25 g/1 oz blue sugarpaste into a ball. Roll the remaining blue sugarpaste into eight thin sausages, tapering the ends to a point, and mark on small circles. Place the tentacles onto the cake as shown, then place the octopus's head on top. Model a cylindrical shape for a clownfish from 25 g/1 oz orange sugarpaste. Shape flat orange fins, outlined with strips of black and white sugarpaste, mark with a knife and press in place. Make black and white eyes for the clownfish and octopus and press in place, then mark on mouths with a skewer. Cut out stars and mark on dots with a skewer to make starfish and model seashells from the white and orange sugarpastes, and dust lightly with gold lustre powder. Roll the green sugarpaste into thin strips and twist for seaweed. Roll out the pink sugarpaste and cut out holes with the top of an icing nozzle or a small, clean bottle cap for coral. Re-roll the scraps and make small coloured cones. Stick everything in place and finish with small candles pushed into scraps of pink sugarpaste.

Smiling Crocodile

Serves 25

For the cake base:

1 x 30 x 25 cm/12 x 10 inch all-in-one
quick-mix slab cake (*see* page 31)
2 bought mini Swiss rolls

To decorate:

chocolate mint stick sweets
2¹/₂ batches vanilla buttercream
25 g/1 oz red and 50 g/2 oz black
ready-to roll sugarpaste
icing sugar, for dusting
emerald green and leaf green paste
food colourings
2 large and 2 mini white
marshmallows
3 tbsp white royal icing (*see* page 50)
or 1 small tube white royal icing
125 g/4 oz golden granulated sugar
18 green jelly sweets

Cut the cake into a body, tail and four leg pieces, following the pattern on page 245. Assemble the pieces on a large board or tray, then secure the pieces together with chocolate stick sweets. Place the mini Swiss rolls in the centre of the head and stick on with a little buttercream. Roll out the black and red sugarpastes on a surface dusted with icing sugar to two thin strips, long enough to go round the mouth of the crocodile. Stick the black one round the mouth and the red one on top, as shown, with a little buttercream.

Colour three quarters of the buttercream emerald green and the remainder leaf green. Place the leaf green buttercream in a large piping bag fitted with a star nozzle and pipe stars onto the back of the body and tail filling in all the spaces. Fill the bag with the emerald green buttercream and pipe stripes around all the edges and all over the rest of the body as shown.

Position the 2 large marshmallows in front of the Swiss rolls and the 2 smaller ones at the front of the head for nostrils, then stick black sugarpaste circles onto them as shown. Place the royal icing in a small paper icing bag fitted with a straight nozzle or pipe from the tube onto the mouth area to make triangular pointed teeth. Pipe white dots onto the eyes.

Scatter the granulated sugar round the animal for sand, then stick the green jelly sweets in place for claws by the feet and onto the back of the body and tail for spines. Finish by piping over any areas that need an extra layer of green buttercream.

Friendly Octopus Cake

Serves 12

For the cake base:

1 x 20 cm/8 inch, all-in-one quick-mix sponge cake (*see* page 30)

To decorate:

1 batch vanilla buttercream
blue, orange, yellow, green, pink and red paste food colourings
350 g/12 oz ready-to-roll sugarpaste
black food colouring pen

Trim the top of the cake level if it has peaked. Brush away any loose crumbs, then place in the freezer for 30 minutes – this will make it easier to spread with the buttercream. Colour the buttercream bright blue and, using a palette knife, spread it over the cake in an even layer. You may find it easier to spread the cake with a thin layer to begin with, then cover this with a second, thicker layer. Smooth as neatly as you can.

Colour 125 g/4 oz sugarpaste bright blue and roll a piece into a walnut-size ball to make the head of the octopus, flattening it slightly. Shape eight legs, rolling thin sausages about 4 cm/1½ inches long. Reserve the remaining blue sugarpaste. Shape two tiny pieces of white sugarpaste into circles for the eyes, mark a black pupil on each with the black food colouring pen, dampen and press into place on the head. Position the head in the centre of the cake and arrange the legs on either side, twisting them as you press them into position.

Divide the remaining sugarpaste into five equal pieces and colour the pieces orange, yellow, green, pink and red. Pull off small pieces of each, including the reserved blue, and shape or stamp into thin circles measuring about 1 cm/½ inch across – you need about 16 circles in total. Press these over the top and sides of the cake. Roll the remaining pieces of coloured sugarpaste into balls about the size of a large pea, dampen and press them around the base of the cake so they are touching.

Ladybird Cake

Serves 20

For the cake base:

1 x 23 cm/9 inch, all-in-one quick-mix sponge (*see* page 30)
450 g/1 lb apricot glaze
1 x 15 cm/6 inch, round all-in-one quick-mix sponge

To decorate:

1.7 kg/3³/₄ lb ready-to-roll sugarpaste
blue, red, black and green paste food colourings
icing sugar, for dusting
¹/₂ batch vanilla buttercream
confectioner's glaze

Trim the top of the large cake level if it has peaked, then brush half the apricot glaze over the top and sides of the cake. Colour 900 g/2 lb of the sugarpaste pale blue and use to cover the large cake (*see* page 62). Transfer to a cake board or plate. Trim the smaller cake into a dome shape, then cut a ridge down the centre for the ladybird's body. Brush the remaining apricot glaze over the cake. Colour 400 g/14 oz sugarpaste red and use to cover the smaller cake. Spread the centre of the larger cake with buttercream and lift the smaller cake on top. Reserve a very small amount of the remaining sugarpaste and colour half of the rest black and half green.

Roll out the green sugarpaste and cut out blades of grass with a sharp knife. Dampen and press them around the bottom edge of the larger cake. Shape the ladybird's head from a ball of black sugarpaste. Shape two antennae, stick onto the head with edible glue and leave to set. Shape six legs and brush these and the head and antennae with confectioner's glaze. Cut out about 12 thin circles from black sugarpaste, 1 cm/¹/₂ inch in diameter. Dampen and press over the body. Shape two small pieces of white sugarpaste into circles for eyes, with smaller black pieces for pupils, dampen and press into place. Shape a mouth from a small sausage of white sugarpaste. Colour a tiny amount of white sugarpaste pink using just a dot of red colouring and roll into two balls. Dampen the mouth and press into place with the two small balls of pink sugarpaste at each end. Fix the head and legs in place with a little cold boiled water. Colour the remaining buttercream green, spoon it into a piping bag fitted with a fine plain nozzle and pipe wiggly lines around the base of the ladybird for 'grass' to finish.

Lazy Giraffe Cake

Serves 16

For the cake base:

1 x 20 cm/8 inch, round, all-in-one
quick-mix sponge mixture baked
in an oval cake tin measuring
about 24 x 17 cm/9¹/₂ x 6¹/₂ inches
rectangular cake card measuring
about 33 x 23 cm/13 x 9 inches
6 tbsp apricot glaze

To decorate:

1.4 kg/3 lb ready-to-roll sugarpaste
icing sugar, for dusting
red, brown, blue and orange paste
food colourings
black sugarcraft pen
¹/₂ batch royal icing (see page 50)

Trim the top of the cake level if it has peaked. Lift it onto the cake card and brush the top and sides with the apricot glaze. Brush the board around the cake with a little water so the overlap of sugarpaste will stick to it. Roll out 900 g/2 lb of the sugarpaste on a board dusted with icing sugar and use to cover the cake (see page 62). Press down some overlap onto the board, trimming it neatly. Using a scroll-patterned embossing tool, mark a pattern all over the sugarpaste. Leave for 12 hours, or longer, until firm.

Colour a quarter of the remaining sugarpaste deep red, roll out and, using small cutters of different sizes, stamp out 20 flowers and 20 hearts. Press a cocktail stick in the centre of each flower and hollow out the centres of the hearts with a sugarcraft bone tool. Colour the remaining sugarpaste light brown and shape an oblong about 9 cm/3¹/₂ inches long for the giraffe's head. Shape as shown, smoothing a sugarcraft ball tool over it where necessary, and make a cut for the mouth. Once firm, use a small paintbrush and dark brown colouring to highlight the mouth, and lighter brown colour to paint on the nostrils. Shape two circles of white sugarpaste for the eyes, dampen and press in place. Draw on eyebrows, eyelashes and pupils using a black sugarcraft pen. Colour two pinhead-size pieces of sugarpaste blue and press onto each pupil. Shape two tiny horns and fix on the head with cold boiled water. Roll out the remaining light brown sugarpaste to a sausage about 23 cm/9 inches long for the neck and arrange it as shown. Fix the neck and head in place with royal icing. Shape two small ears, dampen and press on the sides of the head. Leave until the neck has set firm before painting on markings with orange colouring. Finally, fix the flowers and hearts in place with a little royal icing.

Buzzy Bee Cupcakes

Makes 12

1 batch chocolate cupcakes
(*see* page 33)

To decorate:

1 batch vanilla buttercream
green, hot pink, pale lavender,
yellow and black paste food
colourings
200 g/7 oz ready-to-roll sugarpaste
icing sugar, for dusting

Trim the tops of the cupcakes if they have peaked during baking. Colour the buttercream green and spoon into a large piping bag fitted with a medium plain nozzle. Pipe random lines and swirls backwards and forwards over the cupcakes to cover the tops almost to the edge.

Reserve a small piece of the sugarpaste for the bees' wings. Divide the rest of the sugarpaste into four equal pieces and colour them hot pink, pale lavender, yellow and black. Roll out the hot pink and lavender sugarpaste separately on a board dusted with icing sugar and cut out 12 blossoms from each, using a six-petal flower cutter, about 2.5 cm/ 1 inch across. Roll tiny pieces of yellow sugarpaste into balls, flatten them, dampen the base of each and press into the centre of the blossoms. Arrange a blossom of each colour on top of the cupcakes, pressing them down gently into the buttercream.

Shape 12 ovals, about 2.5 cm/1 inch long, from the yellow sugarpaste to make the bees' bodies. Wrap two strips of black sugarpaste around each, dampening the undersides to fix them in place. Roll 24 small rounds from black sugarpaste, dampen and press into place for eyes. Roll 12 small sausages of black sugarpaste, flatten, dampen and press into place for smiley mouths. Shape 24 wings from the reserved white sugarpaste, dampen and press two on the back of each bee. Brush the underside of each bee with water and position in the centre of the cupcakes, or fix in place with a dab of buttercream.

Cheeky Mice Cake

Serves 8–10

For the cake base:

1 x 18 cm/7 inch, square chocolate
sponge cake (*see* page 27)

To decorate:

1½ batches cream cheese frosting
(*see* page 44)
yellow, pink and purple paste
food colouring
225 g/8 oz ready-to-roll sugarpaste

Trim the top of the cake flat if it has peaked. Colour the cream cheese frosting yellow and liberally spread over the top and sides of the cake, making it as smooth as you can. Place on a flat plate or board and press a round item such as a plastic bottle top into the frosting a few times to give a holey effect.

Reserving a little white for the eyes, colour 75 g/3 oz sugarpaste pink and the rest purple. Take a small piece (less than one quarter) of each, colour a darker shade and reserve.

Model the mice as shown using a ball about two thirds of each lighter colour for the bodies, small flattened balls for the ears and the rest for the heads. Make the eyes from tiny balls of the reserved white sugarpaste, and pupils, noses, legs and tails made from sausages of the darker shade of sugarpaste attaching, them with a little cold boiled water.

Place the mice on the corner of the cake and press a scraping of cream cheese frosting in their paws to finish.

Beautiful Butterfly Cake

Serves 30
(including the cupcakes)

For the cupcakes:
1 batch vanilla cupcakes
(*see* page 33)

To decorate:
white paper
1 batch royal icing using packet mix
pink, yellow and blue paste food
colourings
1 batch vanilla buttercream

For the large cake:
1 x 30 x 25 x 5 cm/12 x 10 x 2 inch all-
in-one quick-mix sponge slab cake
(*see* page 31)

To decorate:
$^1/_2$ batch vanilla buttercream
900 g/2 lb light pink, 175 g/6 oz dark
pink, 125 g/4 oz light yellow,
175g/6 oz dark yellow and 125 g/
4 oz blue ready-to-roll sugarpaste
icing sugar, for dusting

To make the small butterflies, draw round the pattern on page 251 onto a sheet of white paper. Place the paper under a sheet of waxed paper. Divide the royal icing between four bowls, leave one white and colour the remaining icing pink, yellow and blue. Place the white icing in a paper icing bag fitted with a no 1 straight nozzle and carefully pipe round the outline of 12 sets of wings, making a neat join. Add a few drops of water to each of the colours to make a runny consistency. Place a no 2 straight nozzle in a small paper icing bag and fill with blue icing. Pipe the icing into the wings outline, flooding and spreading to the edges. Repeat with the pink and yellow icing, to make four of each. While the icing is still wet, pipe different-coloured dots onto the wings, then leave to dry for 3 hours. Colour the buttercream pink, place in a large piping bag fitted with a star nozzle and pipe onto the cupcakes in swirls. Peel away the waxed paper from the wings. Pipe a body onto each cupcake with the remaining white icing, then place two wings in each.

For the large cake, cut the cake into the shape illustrated on page 244. Spread all over with buttercream. Roll out the light pink sugarpaste on a surface dusted with icing sugar and use to cover the cake (*see* page 62). Place on a cake board. Following the design on page 244, roll and cut out the dark pink, yellow and blue sugarpastes to decorate the wings. Roll out all the remaining sugarpaste pieces thinly and stamp out large, medium and small daisies with a daisy stamp. Dampen all the shapes lightly with a little cold boiled water and press into position as shown.

Monkey Island Cake

Serves 30

For the cake base:

1 x 20 cm/8 inch, round
Madeira cake (see page 28)
1 x 15 cm/6 inch, round
Madeira cake

To decorate:

1/2 batch vanilla buttercream
1.2 kg/2 1/2 lb ready-to-roll sugarpaste
green, brown, red and yellow paste
food colourings
icing sugar, for dusting
700 g/1 1/2 lb marzipan
small tubes black and red
piping icing
thin liquorice sticks

Cut the tops of the cakes level if they have peaked, then cut each in half. Sandwich back together with a little buttercream, then spread the remaining buttercream thinly over the outsides. Colour all but a small piece of the sugarpaste bright green. Roll out 700 g/1 1/2 lb on a surface dusted with icing sugar and use to cover the large cake (see page 62). Use 450 g/1 lb to cover the small cake. Place the small cake on a 15 cm/6 inch, thin cake board, place on top of the large cake and mark all over with the back of a fork. Push green scraps through a garlic press to make grass and press round the bases of both cakes.

Colour 350 g/12 oz of the marzipan brown, 125 g/4 oz beige, 50 g/2 oz red, 125 g/4 oz yellow and 50 g/2 oz green. Model the yellow into bunches of bananas, open banana skins and a snake. Use white sugarpaste or plain marzipan to fashion pieces of 'peeled' banana to stick onto open banana skins. Make two large and four small monkeys. Roll round body pieces and long, thin sausages for arms, legs and tails. Make beige ovals and stick to the body parts. Make brown and beige heads, beige ears and beige mouths and cut across to open them. Roll small white balls for eyes and red strips for tongues. Pipe small black dots on the eyes and mark nostrils on the faces with a skewer. Assemble as shown, then place on the cake with the bananas.

Roll the remaining brown marzipan into long, thin strips and wrap around the liquorice sticks to make tree trunks. Bend and place on the cake, securing with cocktail sticks. Make green marzipan palm leaves, snipping the edges with scissors, and press onto the trees. Roll long, thin, green sausages for vines and red and yellow scraps to stamp out thin daisies. Arrange all as shown.

Farmyard Friends Cupcakes

Makes 20

For the cakes:

1½ batches (to make 20 small)
chocolate cupcakes
(*see* page 33)
4 tbsp apricot glaze

To decorate:

1.1 kg/2 lb 6 oz ready-to-roll
sugarpaste
green, pink, yellow and brown
paste food colourings
icing sugar, for dusting
black sugarcraft pen

Trim the tops of the cupcakes if they have peaked, then brush over the apricot glaze. Colour 350 g/12 oz sugarpaste pale green and roll out on a board dusted with icing sugar. Using a fluted cutter slightly larger than the tops of the cupcakes, stamp out 12 circles and press into place.

To make the animal decorations, divide the remaining sugarpaste into four pieces (one of which is slightly bigger than the rest) and colour one pink, one yellow and one brown, leaving the bigger piece white.

Roll out all the sugarpastes thinly. Using the photograph as a guide for colours and the templates on page 249 as a guide for shapes, cut out four bodies and heads of each animal (pig, sheep, cow, horse and chicken), and the appropriate number of ears, snouts and beaks. Roll tiny sausages of brown sugarpaste for the chicken nests. Dampen the pieces with cold boiled water and press on top of the cupcakes.

Draw on facial features, body markings and hooves where appropriate with a black sugarcraft pen. Use a cocktail stick to mark nostrils and mane and tail textures.

Finish by adding tiny coloured dots of sugarpaste onto some of the animals, fixing them in place with a dab of water.

Fantasy & Adventure

Kids have boundless imaginations and an appetite for dreaming up all kinds of fantasy worlds and adventures; pirate ship missions and magic genies to angels and princesses and everything in between. With these fantastic projects, you can bring these imaginary worlds to life in cake form. The Colourful Candyland Cake is a dream come true for sweetie fans, whilst the Princess Castle Cake is the epitome of perfection for aspiring royalty.

Regal Rose Cupcakes

Makes 12

For the cakes:

1 batch vanilla cupcakes
(*see* page 33)
4 tbsp apricot glaze

To decorate:

700 g/1½ lb ready-to-roll
sugarpaste
pink, green and yellow paste food
colourings
icing sugar, for dusting
edible glue
white and yellow sugar sprinkles

Trim the tops of the cupcakes level if they have peaked, then brush over the apricot glaze. Colour 500 g/1 lb 2 oz sugarpaste deep pink. Reserve 150 g/5 oz and roll out the rest on a board dusted with icing sugar. Using a plain cutter the same size as the tops of the cupcakes, stamp out 12 circles and press one circle on top of each cupcake, smoothing it down neatly.

Use the reserved pink sugarpaste to model six roses (*see* page 63). Colour half the remaining sugarpaste pale green, roll out and cut out 24 leaves with a cutter or small, sharp knife. Mark a vein down the centre of each leaf with a knife or cocktail stick, taking care not to cut the leaves in half.

Colour the rest of the sugarpaste yellow, roll out thinly and cut out six strips measuring about 6.5 cm/2½ inches long by 2 cm/¾ inch wide. Using a small, sharp knife, cut 'V' shapes into one long edge of each to make the tops of the crowns. Curl each strip round in a circle and stick the ends together with edible glue.

Brush the edges of the sugarpaste covering the cupcakes with edible glue and press on the sugar sprinkles. Stick the crowns in the centre of six cupcakes with edible glue, brush the bottom edges of the crowns with more glue and press sprinkles around each. Stick the roses and the leaves on top of the remaining cupcakes with edible glue to finish.

One-Eyed Pirate Cake

Serves 10–12

For the cake base:

1 x 13 cm/5 inch, square almond
Madeira cake baked in a 2 litre/
4 pint bowl (*see* page 28)
4 tbsp apricot glaze

To decorate:

1.3 kg/2³/₄ lb ready-to-roll
sugarpaste
flesh, red and black paste food
colourings
icing sugar, for dusting

Trim the top of the cake level if it has peaked, then brush the apricot glaze over the domed side of the cake. Colour 900 g/2 lb sugarpaste flesh toned, roll it out on a board dusted with icing sugar and use to cover the cake (*see* page 62). Gather up the trimmings and roll two small balls about 1 cm/¹/₂ inch in diameter. Flatten the balls with your fingers to make a nose and left ear, dampen the underside and side respectively and press in place.

Colour two thirds of the remaining sugarpaste red to make the headscarf and roll out very thinly to a semicircle large enough to fit over the top third of the cake. Trim the bottom edge of the semicircle straight, dampen the underside and lift into position, smoothing it down, then trim. Using the trimmings, roll a small ball about 1 cm/¹/₂ inch in diameter. Roll out a small piece of the paste and cut a strip, 2.5 cm/1 inch wide. Cut a 'V' shape into one end of the strip. Dampen both the ball and the strip and press into place to make the knot at the end of the pirate's scarf. Roll out half the remaining sugarpaste very thinly and cut out eight circles, 1.5 cm/³/₄ inch in diameter (if you don't have a cutter this size, use the base of a small icing nozzle). Dampen the undersides and press into position over the pirate's scarf.

Cut another slightly smaller round measuring about 1 cm/¹/₂ inch for the eye, dampen and fix into place. Colour the rest of the sugarpaste black and roll out very thinly. Cut out a long, thin strip and a round for the eye patch and a small, heart-shaped piece for the pupil, dampen and press into place. Using the tip of a sharp knife, mark the pirate's mouth to finish.

Magic Garden Cake

Serves 20

For the cake base:

1 x 15 cm/6 inch, round lemon
Madeira cake (*see* page 28)
1 x 23 cm/9 inch, round lemon
Madeira cake
6 tbsp apricot glaze

To decorate:

15 cm/6 inch, round cake board
1.8 kg/4 lb ready-to-roll sugarpaste
blue, green, pink, yellow and purple
paste food colourings
icing sugar, for dusting
edible silver balls
black and green sugarcraft pens

Trim the tops of the cakes level if they have peaked, then brush the apricot glaze over the cakes. Colour 450 g/1 lb sugarpaste pale blue and use to cover the small cake. Trim the bottom neatly and lift the cake onto the cake card. Colour 900 g/2 lb sugarpaste pale green and use to cover the larger cake. Transfer this to a board or plate and put the smaller cake on top. Colour the trimmings of pale blue sugarpaste a deeper shade of blue. Roll into balls, about the size of a small pea, dampen these with cold boiled water and press them around the base of the smaller cake. Colour the trimmings of pale green sugarpaste a deeper shade of green.

Colour half the remaining sugarpaste deep pink and roll out a strip 1 cm/ 1/2 inch wide and long enough to go around the large cake. Mark lines along the edges of the strip, dampen and press around the base of the cake. Colour small pieces of the remaining sugarpaste pale pink, yellow and pale purple, leaving one piece white. Cut leaves and flower stalks from the green sugarpaste, then cut flowers from the pink or white sugarpaste and butterflies from the purple sugarpaste using butterfly cutters. Dampen the cut-outs and position as shown. Add flower centres using white or pink sugarpaste and details on the butterflies using yellow, pink and blue sugarpaste. Shape bees from yellow and white sugarpastes and press around the sides of the larger cake. Draw antennae on the butterflies (with edible silver balls on the tips) using a black sugarcraft pen and small trails of dots around the butterflies with a green pen, and mark lines on the wings with a knife. Add details to the flowers with the black pen and on the leaves with the green pen to finish.

Sleeping Angel Cake

Serves 40

For the cake base:

1 x 23 cm/9 inch, square
Madeira cake (*see* page 28)
1 x 16 cm/6 inch, square
Madeira cake

To decorate:

1 batch vanilla buttercream
1.8 kg/4 lb ready-to-roll sugarpaste
pink, flesh and brown paste
food colourings
icing sugar, for dusting
2 tbsp royal icing (*see* page 50)

Trim the tops of the cakes if they have peaked. Cut each cake in half horizontally and spread one half with a little buttercream. Place the other layer on top and spread the remaining buttercream over the top and sides of the cakes.

Colour 1.25 kg/2$^1/_2$ lb sugarpaste light pink. Use 875 g/1$^3/_4$ lb pink sugarpaste to cover the large cake (*see* page 62), then place on a 30 cm/12 inch cake board. Repeat to cover the small cake with the remaining pink sugarpaste and place on a thin cake board. Place the small cake on top of the larger one.

Colour 50 g/2 oz sugarpaste flesh toned. Roll half into a ball for the angel's head, two sausages for arms and two tiny balls for feet. Roll 50 g/2 oz white sugarpaste into a triangular shape for the body, then position the pieces onto the small cake as shown. Mark a face on the angel with a skewer, then colour the royal icing brown and place in a piping bag fitted with a no 1 straight nozzle. Pipe strands on the head for hair.

Roll the remaining white sugarpaste out thinly and cut into thin strips 2 cm/$^3/_4$ inch wide. Dampen the underside of each strip with a little cold boiled water and press round the base of the large and small cakes. Make bows (*see* page 63) with trailing ribbons for each of the cake corners. Re-roll the trimmings and cut out small stars with a star cutter, along with two little wings. Stick the stars onto both the cakes as shown, in a cascade, one on top of the angel's head and the wings on her back.

Fairy Dust Flower Cupcakes

Makes 12

For the cakes:

1 batch vanilla cupcakes
(*see* page 33)

To decorate:

125 g/4 oz ready-to-roll sugarpaste
pink and blue paste food colourings
icing sugar, for dusting
1 batch vanilla buttercream
25 g/1 oz granulated sugar

Colour 25 g/1 oz sugarpaste deep pink and the remainder blue. Roll out the blue sugarpaste on a board or surface dusted with icing sugar and cut out 12 daisies using a medium daisy cutter. Mould the pink sugarpaste into 12 small balls and mark the centre of each with the tip of a small knife to represent the centre of a flower. Press the petals upwards to curl them, then lightly dampen the underside of each pink centre and press into the daisies. Leave to dry for 1 hour on nonstick baking parchment.

Colour the buttercream pale pink and the granulated sugar a deeper shade of pink with a little pink paste food colouring.

Place the pink buttercream in a large piping bag fitted with a plain nozzle. Pipe a plain swirl round the outside of each cupcake, then fill in the centre by piping a large round swirl.

Just before serving, spread the pink sugar out onto a saucer and dip the outside of each cake in the sugar, lightly coating round all the sides. Place a daisy in the centre of each cake to finish.

Princess Castle Cake

୧

Serves 40–50

For the cake base:

2 x 12 cm/5 inch Madeira cakes
2 x 20 cm/8 inch Madeira cakes

To decorate:

hundreds and thousands
5 ice-cream cones
¹/₄ batch royal icing (*see* page 50)
3¹/₂ batches vanilla buttercream,
coloured pale pink
150 g/5 oz ready-to-roll sugarpaste
cream paste food colouring
Iced Gems
jelly sweets
50 g/2 oz desiccated coconut
green liquid food colouring
coloured paper and cocktail sticks,
for the flags

Pour the hundreds and thousands out on a sheet of nonstick baking parchment. Coat the ice-cream cones with royal icing and roll them in the hundreds and thousands to cover.

Trim the tops of the cakes flat if they have peaked and sandwich them together in pairs with a small amount of buttercream to make deep cakes. Cover both cakes with the remaining buttercream and mark lines in it with a fork as shown. Place the larger cake on a 30 cm/12 inch cake board and the smaller cake on a thin, 12 cm/5 inch, square cake board and place it on top of the larger cake.

Colour the sugarpaste cream, then roll long, thin sausages to go round the bases of the cakes and press into place. Roll out and cut out a square of sugarpaste for the gate. Press this into place and make the drawbridge from thin sausages of sugarpaste as shown.

Position the decorated ice-cream cones, Iced Gems and jelly sweets around the cake as shown.

Put the desiccated coconut in a bowl and, while stirring, add drops of green food colouring until the desired colour is achieved. Scatter the coconut around the edge of the board. Add flags made from coloured paper stuck on cocktail sticks – why not add a name or message on them too? Push the flags into the tops of the cones to finish.

Colourful Candyland Cake

Serves 80

For the cake base:

1 each 15 cm/6 inch, 20 cm/8 inch
and 25 cm/10 inch, round
Madeira cake (see page 28)

To decorate:

1¹/₂ batches vanilla buttercream
3 kg/6 lb 6 oz ready-to-roll
sugarpaste
icing sugar, for dusting
yellow, pink, blue, purple, green
and red paste food colourings
candles

Trim the top of the cakes flat if they have peaked and spread the buttercream over the top and sides. Colour 1.7 kg/3 lb 11 oz sugarpaste yellow and use to cover the cakes (see page 62). Place the small cake on a 15 cm/6 inch thin cake board, the medium cake on a 20 cm/8 inch thin cake board and stack the cakes on a large board (see page 69).

Colour 700 g/1¹/₂ lb sugarpaste pink, roll one third into a ball and roll out on a board dusted with icing sugar. Cut a circle slightly larger than the top cake and use fluted cutter or pastry wheel to cut semicircles from the edges as shown. Dampen the top of the cake with a cold boiled water and drape over the pink circle, easing it down the sides. Repeat with strips of pink sugarpaste to cover the visible top edges of each cake. Reserve the offcuts.

Use 150 g/5 oz white sugarpaste to model the two cats as shown (or use a mould if you have one). Keeping some of it white for details, colour the remaining sugarpaste in batches of blue, purple, green and a little red. Roll these out, then cut out the doors and windows on the castle as shown and attach with a little cold boiled water. Press markings into them with a knife and star stamps. Add coloured details to the cats.

Use up all the offcuts, creating spirals and balls topped with a white cut-out daisy and coloured centre. Press these onto wooden skewers and push into balls of green sugarpaste around the board. Add candles to finish.

Princess ❧ the Frog Cake

Serves 10–12

For the cake base:

1 x 22 cm/9 inch, round all-in-one
quick-mix sponge made in a
pudding basin (see page 32)

To decorate:

1.25 kg/2 lb 13 oz ready-to-roll
sugarpaste
green, pink, purple and yellow
paste food colourings
1/2 batch vanilla buttercream

Colour 30 g/1¹/4 oz sugarpaste green and model a 4 cm/1¹/2 inch high frog, marking the features with a knife and adding tiny balls of white for the eyes. Colour 100 g/3¹/2 oz sugarpaste deep pink and 900 g/2 lb sugarpaste light purple. Make 12 tiny, 1 cm/¹/2 inch pink roses (see page 63). Use the rest of the pink and a little of the purple to model the crowns as shown, supporting them with balls of clingfilm or cotton wool while drying.

Trim the top of the cake flat if it has peaked and turn upside down. Spread the buttercream over the top and sides. Place on a large cake board or flat plate. Roll 750 g/1¹/2 lb purple sugarpaste to a 40 cm/16 inch round and lift onto the cake loosely, lifting and crimping the paste to fall into gentle folds. Tuck and trim round the base. Take 100 g/3¹/2 oz of the purple sugarpaste and model it into the shape of the body. Attach two smaller balls on each side with a little cold boiled water and stick the torso on top of the cake.

Colour two thirds of the remaining sugarpaste pale pink and the rest yellow. Model the head and arms and stick these, together with the frog, into place. Model locks of yellow hair and paint features on the faces using the black and purple colourings and a very fine-tipped paintbrush.

Roll the remaining purple sugarpaste and offcuts into thin strands and, with a little water, stick them round the bottom of the dress in groups of three to create the swags. Add a sugar rose between each swag to finish.

Dream Carousel Cake

Serves 10–12

For the cake base:

1 x 22 cm/9 inch, round Madeira
cake (see page 28)

To decorate:

450 g/1 lb flower paste
1.1 kg/2 lb 6 oz ready-to-roll
sugarpaste
pink, green and brown paste
food colourings
stiff white card
icing sugar, for dusting
1/2 batch vanilla buttercream
3 white plastic cake dowels
1/2 batch royal icing (see page 50)
bought fabric flowers and ribbons

Using the flower paste and a silicon mould (see page 55) make three horses. Leave to dry. Colour the sugarpaste pink.

Cut a 25 cm/10 inch diameter circle out of stiff white card and cut a slit into the centre. Overlap the cut edges slightly and staple or stick together to create a shallow cone that will fit on a thin, 22 cm/9 inch cake board. Secure it to the board with a couple of balls of pink sugarpaste. Roll out 300 g/ 11 oz pink sugarpaste on a surface dusted with icing sugar and cover the cone and the edge of the board. Trim and crimp a pattern around the edge.

Trim the top of the cake flat if it has peaked and spread the buttercream over the top and sides. Use the remaining sugarpaste to cover the cake (see page 68). Place on a 28 cm/11 inch cake board and crimp a design to match the roof.

Make a cylinder of white card to fit in the centre of the cake and press this and three white plastic cake dowels into place onto the top of the cake.

Colour dessertspoonfuls of royal icing pale green, deep pink and brown and pipe the tiny leaves, deep pink swags (on the roof) and a message. Colour the remaining royal icing pink and add the pale swags, then attach all the ribbons and flowers with it as shown. Prop the horses in place, balance the roof on top and add a ribbon and bow around the base to finish.

Secret Garden Cupcakes

Makes 12

For the cakes:

! batch vanilla cupcakes
(*see* page 33)

To decorate:

75 g/3 oz ready-to-roll sugarpaste
pink and green paste food colourings
icing sugar, for dusting
1 batch vanilla buttercream
2 tbsp royal icing (*see* page 50)
coloured pink, or a small tube of
pink royal icing

Colour 25 g/1 oz sugarpaste deep pink, 25 g/1 oz light pink and leave the remainder white. Roll out the deep pink paste on a board or surface dusted with icing sugar and cut out 12 daisies using a medium daisy stamp. Press the petals upwards to curl them, then leave to dry for 1 hour on nonstick baking parchment.

Trim the tops of the cakes flat if they have peaked. Colour the buttercream bright green, then place in a paper piping bag fitted with a leaf nozzle and pipe small green leaves all over the top of each cake, carefully filling in all the spaces. Place a deep pink, light pink and white daisy in the centre of each cake.

To finish, place the royal icing in a small paper piping bag fitted with a plain nozzle, or use a piping tube, and pipe a small dot in the centre of each daisy.

Genie Lamp Cake

Serves 18

For the cake base:

1 x 22 cm/8¹/₂ inch square
Madeira cake (*see* page 28)

To decorate:

¹/₂ batch vanilla buttercream
1.2 kg/2 lb 10 oz ready-to-roll
sugarpaste
pink, brown, blue and purple paste
food colourings
pink spray food colouring (optional)
icing sugar, for dusting
gold lustre powder
³/₄ batch royal icing (*see* page 50)
blue ribbon frill

Trim the top of the cake flat if it has peaked and spread with buttercream.

Colour 1 kg/2¹/₄ lb sugarpaste pink and use it to cover the cake, following the instructions on page 62, then place on a 30 cm/12 inch cake board. If liked, spray pink colouring around the sides of the cake, and leave to dry.

Colour the remaining sugarpaste light brown. Roll out thinly on a surface dusted with icing sugar and, using the template (*see* page 250), cut out the lamp shape. Dust with gold lustre powder and lift onto the cake. When you are happy with the positioning, lift up a few edges and brush a little cold boiled water underneath to stick the lamp to the cake.

Colour a small amount of royal icing light brown and, using a fine writing nozzle, pipe the details on the lamp.

Colour one third of the royal icing blue. Using a medium writing nozzle, pipe the curlicque design around the cake, plus the dots on the lamp as shown. Attach the ribbon frill around the base of the cake (*see* page 64 if you prefer to make the frill from sugarpaste).

Colour the remaining royal icing purple and, using a star nozzle, pipe shells around the base of the cake. Use the last bit in a small paper piping bag (*see* page 58) to pipe the purple dots on the lamp. Lightly brush gold lustre powder on the piping around the lamp to finish.

Pretty Princess Cake

❦

Serves 8–12

For the cake base:

1 x 18 cm/7 inch, round rich chocolate cake (*see* page 27)

To decorate:

¼ batch chocolate buttercream
1.1 kg/2 lb 8 oz ready-to-roll sugarpaste
brown, cream, flesh, chestnut, pink and black paste food colourings
1 Walnut Whip
icing sugar, for dusting
4 silver or pearl dragees
6 candles

Trim the top of the cake flat if it has peaked and spread the buttercream over the top and sides. Colour 600 g/1 lb 5 oz sugarpaste brown and use to cover the cake (*see* page 62). Trim (reserving the offcuts) and place on a 25 cm/10 inch, square cake board. Remove the walnut from the Walnut Whip, trim the bottom edge inwards and chill to avoid a sticky mess!

Colour 165 g/5½ oz of the sugarpaste cream, 100 g/3½ oz flesh toned, 40 g/1½ oz chestnut brown and 250 g/9 oz pink. Roll out 25 g/1 oz of the cream sugarpaste on a board or surface dusted with icing sugar, then cut out hearts and stick to the cake with a little cold boiled water. Roll half the remaining cream sugarpaste into a ball, flatten, roll out and quickly wrap around the Walnut Whip, covering it. Place it in the centre of the cake for the body and press the pearl dragees down the front. Take a ball of the flesh sugarpaste, model the head, creating features with bits of pink and brown, and stick on top of the body with cold boiled water. Using the remaining cream and flesh sugarpastes, model the rest of the figure as shown, starting with the legs, then the skirt, sleeves and arms. Use the chestnut sugarpaste for the hair and paint on the eyes with black food colouring.

Using the pink sugarpaste, roll out a strip to fit around the base of the cake and press into place. Use the rest to make a bow (*see* page 63) and press into place. Model a tiny pair of wings with any pink offcuts and place on the board. Press six candles into balls of the brown sugarpaste offcuts and place around the board to finish.

Vintage Style Cupcakes

Makes 24

For the cakes:

2 batches vanilla cupcakes
(*see* page 33)

To decorate:

125 g/4 oz ready-to-roll sugarpaste
2 batches vanilla buttercream
pink paste food colouring
selection of pearls and small jewels

Roll the sugarpaste until flexible, then take a pea-size ball and roll into a cone shape. Take another ball and flatten out into a petal shape. Wrap the petal round the cone and continue to add petals to make an open rose (*see* page 63). Trim the base and leave to dry in an egg box lined with crumpled foil for 2 hours to firm. Make three roses.

Trim the tops of the cakes flat if they have peaked. Colour the buttercream a delicate pale pink then place half in a large piping bag fitted with a large star nozzle. Pipe the buttercream onto the cakes in large swirls. Refill the bag and continue piping onto all the cakes.

Place the cupcakes on a large tray or flat serving platter in the shape of a dress, then place the roses in a belt arrangement with the pearls and jewels, as shown.

Tiered Princess Birthday Cake

Serves 20

For the cake base:

1 x 15 cm/6 inch, round almond
Madeira cake (*see* page 28)
1 x 23 cm/9 inch, round almond
Madeira cake
6 tbsp apricot glaze

To decorate:

1.8 kg/4 lb ready-to-roll sugarpaste
blue, purple and pink paste food
colourings
15 cm/6 inch, round cake card
icing sugar, for dusting
small quantity blue royal icing

Trim the tops of the cakes level if they have peaked, then brush the apricot glaze over the cakes. Colour 1.4 kg/3 lb sugarpaste blue. Roll out two thirds on a board dusted with icing sugar and use to cover the larger cake (*see* page 62). Trim the bottom neatly and transfer the cake to a board or plate. Cover the smaller cake in the same way with blue sugarpaste and lift it onto the cake card. Lift the smaller cake on top of the larger one.

Colour half the remaining sugarpaste purple and half deep pink. Roll out the purple and, using a small, sharp knife, cut out diamonds the same size as the depth of the smaller cake. Dampen the diamonds and press them around the sides of the cake so they are just touching. Using the templates on page 253 cut out four fairy castle shapes from the purple sugarpaste. Roll out the pink sugarpaste and use the templates, cut out four slippers and one crown. Dampen the castle and slipper shapes and press them alternately around the sides of the larger cake. Dampen the crown shape and press onto the centre of the top of the smaller cake. Cut small triangles from the pink sugarpaste, dampen and press around the top edge of the cake. Roll the remaining pink sugarpaste into pea-size balls, dampen and press around the base of the smaller cake.

Spoon the blue royal icing into a small piping bag fitted with a star nozzle and pipe tiny rosettes between the pink triangles, and shells between the fairy castles and the slippers.

Over the Rainbow Cupcakes

Makes 12

For the cakes:

1 batch vanilla cupcake mixture
(*see* page 33)

To decorate:

red, yellow, green, pink and blue
paste food colourings
flat, thin toffee strips or bought
rainbow strip sweet
caster sugar
150 ml/¼ pint whipping cream

Make up a batch of cupcake mixture (*see* page 33) and divide it between three bowls. Colour one batch red, one yellow and one green.

Line a muffin tray with paper cases and place a layer of green cake mixture in the base of each case. Spoon a layer of yellow mixture on top, then top each case with a layer of red mixture. Bake following the instructions on page 33 until the cakes are well risen and springy to the touch. Cool for a few minutes, then turn out onto a wire rack to cool.

If you are not using bought rainbow strip sweets, cut the strips of toffee into 8 cm/3¼ inch lengths. Carefully paint on red stripes, leave to dry for a few minutes, then paint on yellow, green, pink and blue stripes, allowing the colouring to dry in between. Sprinkle the strips with caster sugar on both sides.

Whip the cream until stiff and place in a piping bag fitted with a plain nozzle. Pipe two blobs onto each cake, then carefully bend the bought rainbow strip sweet or toffee strip over and press into the cream to secure. Serve the cakes within 30 minutes, as the toffee will start to soften.

Ship Ahoy Cake

Serves 14–18

For the cake base:

1 x 30 x 25 x 5 cm/12 x 10 x 2 inch, all-in-one quick-mix slab cake (*see* page 31)

To decorate:

$^1/_2$ batch chocolate buttercream
1.4 kg/3 lb ready-to-roll sugarpaste
brown and blue paste food colourings
icing sugar, for dusting
$^1/_4$ batch royal icing (*see* page 50)
wooden skewers

Cut the cake into three oblongs as shown on page 247 and cut the pieces following the diagram. Spread the pieces with buttercream and assemble to a boat shape as shown. Spread the remaining buttercream over the top and sides of the boat and place on a cake board. Colour 900 g/2 lb sugarpaste brown, 50 g/2 oz dark brown and leave the remainder white. Roll out 125 g/4 oz white sugarpaste thinly on a surface dusted with icing sugar. Cut out three large squares about 8 cm/3 $^1/_4$ inches, and two smaller squares about 5 cm/2 inches and make a hole at the base and top of each square. Cut out a small and a large triangular pennant shape. Cover a rolling pin with clingfilm and place the sails over to make them curve. Leave to dry for 4 hours until firm.

Roll out the brown sugarpaste and use to cover the boat (*see* page 62). Trim and place on a board. Mark a wood effect on the top and sides of the boat using a round-bladed knife. Roll brown trimmings into a long, thin sausage and press this round the top of the boat to make a border. Roll small brown squares and a round for portholes. Decorate these and the prow with darker brown sugarpaste, as shown. Roll out a small white sugarpaste window and stick on, then lightly paint with blue food colouring. Spread half the royal icing on the board around the cake. Roll the remaining white sugarpaste thinly, place on the icing and pinch together to represent waves. Dab with blue food colouring. Roll a scrap of white sugarpaste into an oblong banner, place on the waves and paint on 'Happy Birthday' or another message of your choice with blue food colouring. Thread the sails onto the skewers and place in position. Colour a little royal icing brown and pipe on a ladder and window frame as shown.

Lovestruck Tiered Cake

Serves 20

For the cake base:

1 x 20 cm/8 inch Madeira cake
(*see* page 28)
1 x 15 cm/6 inch Madeira cake

To decorate:

1.75 kg/3¹/₂ lb ready-to-roll
sugarpaste
pink and red paste food colourings
icing sugar, for dusting
¹/₂ batch vanilla buttercream
edible silver balls

Reserve 225 g/8 oz sugarpaste. Divide the remaining sugarpaste into 575 g/1¹/₄ lb and 450 g/1 lb batches. Knead the largest batch until soft, add pink paste colouring, then roll out on a surface dusted with icing sugar to a circle large enough to cover the large cake. Spread the cake with buttercream, then place the sugarpaste over the cake, smooth down over the top and sides and flatten with an icing tool or your palms. Trim the edges, then repeat to cover the smaller cake with the 450 g/ 1 lb white sugarpaste. Place the smaller cake on a 15 cm/6 inch, thin, round cake board and stack the smaller cake on top of the large one.

Colour 50 g/2 oz of the remaining sugarpaste deep pink and 75 g/3 oz red. Roll the pink sugarpaste out thickly and cut out a large heart shape. Leave to harden for 4 hours on nonstick baking parchment.

Roll out the red sugarpaste thinly and cut out a strip 2 cm/³/₄ inch wide. Dampen the underside of the red strip and press round the base of the white cake, pinching the sugarpaste into pleats at intervals as shown. Using a small heart cutter or the pattern on page 252, cut out a small red heart and place at the front of the cake. Roll out the white sugarpaste and stamp out 30 small hearts with a cutter or follow the pattern as above. Dampen the underside of each heart and press round the base of the pink cake to make a border. Press silver balls onto the white cake and press the pink heart into the centre of the top white cake to finish.

Hobbies & Interests

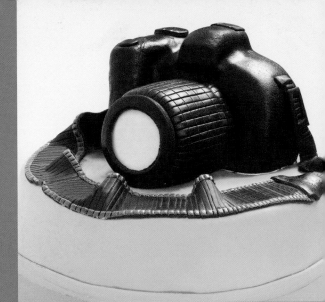

Whether it be photography, dancing, football, trainspotting or even shopping, most children have at least a couple of hobbies or interests to their name. Celebrating these with a themed cake will be much appreciated and will encourage them to keep it up. Fans of the great outdoors will be charmed by the Camping Fun Cake, and budding rugby players will love the Rugby Ball Cupcakes, whilst the Disco Diva Cake would fit in perfectly at any teenage disco.

Cupcake Crazy Cake

Serves 40

For the cake base:

1 x 23 cm/9 inch chocolate cake
(*see* page 27)
1 x 18 cm/7 inch Madeira cake
(*see* page 28)
1 large bought giant cupcake

To decorate:

1¼ batches vanilla buttercream
1.8 kg/4 lb ready-to-roll
sugarpaste
pink and brown paste food
colourings
icing sugar, for dusting
coloured sprinkles
1 glacé cherry
thin angelica or liquorice strip
(optional)
gold lustre powder

Cut the tops of the cakes flat if they have peaked. Spread the tops and sides with buttercream and coat the cupcake lightly with buttercream. Colour 1.25 kg/2½ lb sugarpaste pink and 250 g/12 oz dark brown. Divide the pink sugarpaste into 700 g/1½ lb and 450 g/1 lb batches. Colour the larger batch a darker shade of pink and use to cover the larger cake (*see* page 62). Cover the smaller cake with the lighter pink sugarpaste. Roll 50 g/ 2 oz white sugarpaste into a strip and wrap round the sides of the cupcake.

Place the larger cake on a 15 cm/6 inch, thin, round cake board, and stack the cakes as shown. Colour the remaining buttercream pink and spread over the top of the cupcake, then scatter sprinkles over and top with the glacé cherry (adding a thin strip of angelica or liquorice for the 'stalk', if liked).

Colour white sugarpaste scraps pink to create a marbled effect. Roll into 3 long, thin, strips then coil round into 3 circles. Push a cocktail stick into each circle and leave to dry on nonstick baking parchment for 2 hours until firm. Add a little extra pink colouring to the scraps to make deep pink, then roll into strips along with the brown sugarpaste, dampen the underside of each with a little cold boiled water and press onto the larger cake as shown. Roll the pink sugarpaste scraps into a thin strip, flatten and press round the base. Roll out scraps and cut out white, pink and brown large and small discs and decorate as shown. Roll the remaining sugarpaste into 18 large and 8 small balls in each colour and position as shown. Brush gold lustre powder over some of the strips and balls. Push the lollipops into the cake before serving.

Happy Engine Cake

Serves 14–18

For the cake base:

1 x 20 cm/8 inch, square
chocolate cake (*see* page 27)
1 bought chocolate Swiss roll
1 bought mini Swiss roll

To decorate:

1¹/₂ batches vanilla buttercream
blue, red, yellow and black paste
food colourings
25 g/1 oz ready-to-roll red
sugarpaste
icing sugar, for dusting
15 g/¹/₂ oz ready-to-roll black
sugarpaste
2 bought mini meringues

Cut the cake in half, then cut one half into two squares. Place one square on top of the other, then stack the squares on top of the oblong piece. Cut a curve round the front part of the oblong. Spread the pieces lightly with buttercream and stick in position. Cut the Swiss roll to size if needed, then place on top of the oblong and stick down with buttercream. Cut the mini Swiss roll in half and shape into a chimney funnel and stick in place.

Divide the remaining buttercream into five batches and colour them light blue, dark blue, red, yellow and black.

Roll the red sugarpaste on a surface dusted with icing sugar into a round large enough to cover the front of the engine. Roll the black sugarpaste into a thin sausage between your palms. Cut strips to make a smiley mouth and two eyes as shown and press onto the red sugarpaste. Press the red disc onto the front of the engine.

Place the light blue buttercream in a piping bag fitted with a small star nozzle and pipe stars on to cover the body of the engine. Pipe three wheels on each side of the engine with the blue icing. Clean the bag and refill it with dark blue buttercream and pipe stars on the back of the engine as shown. Clean the bag and refill with black buttercream and fill in the design as shown. Repeat with the red buttercream. Clean the bag and fill with the yellow buttercream and pipe a border of stars round the engine parts as shown. To finish, place small meringues in the chimney funnel as shown, for smoke.

Football Fanatic Cake

Serves 10–12

For the cake base:

20 cm/8 inch, round all-in-one quick-mix sponge (*see* page 30)

To decorate:

¼ batch vanilla buttercream
750 g/1 lb 10 oz ready-to-roll sugarpaste
black paste food colouring
icing sugar, for dusting
red ribbon trim (or ribbons of your team colours)

Trim the top of the cake flat if it has peaked and spread the buttercream over the top and sides. Use 650 g/1 lb 7 oz sugarpaste to cover the cake following the instructions on page 62 and place on a 25 cm/10 inch cake board or plate.

Press the edge of a ruler or the back of a long knife across the top of the cake and then at two diagonals to make the indented pattern markings.

Colour the remaining sugarpaste (and any trimmings) black, roll out thinly on a surface dusted with icing sugar and cut out one hexagon and six half hexagons. Stick these in place on the top of the cake with a little cold boiled water. Arrange the ribbon around the base to finish.

Tea Party Cake

Serves 20

For the cake base:

1 x 23 cm/9 inch, square rich
chocolate cake (*see* page 27)
1 x all-in-one quick-mix sponge
cake baked in a 900 ml/1¹/₂ pint
pudding basin (*see* page 32)

To decorate:

1 batch vanilla buttercream
875 g/1³/₄ lb ready-to-roll chocolate
sugarpaste
icing sugar, for dusting
700 g/1¹/₂ lb ready-to-roll white
sugarpaste
fancy paper napkins
¹/₄ batch royal icing (*see* page 50)
green paste food colouring
bought iced piped flowers, 1 rose
and 3 daisies
thin pink and brown satin
ribbon trim

Cut the top of the square cake flat if it has peaked, then spread with two thirds of the buttercream. Roll out the chocolate sugarpaste on a surface dusted with icing sugar and use to cover the cake (*see* page 62).

Carve the pudding basin cake into a round ball shape with a sharp knife. Spread with the remaining buttercream. Roll out half the white sugarpaste to a circle large enough to completely enclose the ball and use to cover (*see* page 62). Place the ball on the square cake with the join underneath. Model a teapot lid and stick in place with a little cold boiled water.

Roll thick sausages of white sugarpaste and model into a handle and teapot spout. Leave these to dry and harden on nonstick baking parchment for 3 hours until firm. Cover the outside of a small upturned plastic carton or teacup with clingfilm. Roll some white sugarpaste into a small circle and mould over the cup. Repeat with a small upturned saucer covered in clingfilm. Model a handle for the teacup and leave to dry as above. When firm enough, remove the cup and saucer from the moulded sugarpaste.

Roll a small square of sugarpaste and place on the cake with a fancy napkin on top. Cut a border from a matching napkin and stick round the teacup with a dab of royal icing. Stick the teapot handle, spout and teacup handle in place with a little royal icing. Colour the remaining royal icing pale green and place in a paper icing bag fitted with a leaf nozzle. Pipe leaves as shown and add the iced flowers. Attach the ribbon round the base to finish.

My Camera Cake

Serves 18

For the cake base:

1 x 20 cm/8 inch, round
Madeira cake (*see* page 28)
1 x 16 cm/6 inch, square
Madeira cake

To decorate:

¹/₂ batch vanilla buttercream
700 g/1¹/₂ lb ready-to-roll
white sugarpaste
turquoise and pink paste
food colourings
icing sugar, for dusting
350 g/12 oz ready-to-roll black
sugarpaste

Trim the top of the round cake flat if it has peaked and spread lightly with buttercream. Colour 575 g/1¹/₄ lb white sugarpaste turquoise. Roll out on a surface dusted with icing sugar to a circle large enough to cover the cake. Lift over the cake, smooth over and trim the edges. Roll the trimmings into a thin strip and press round the base of the cake.

Cut the square cake in half and, following the diagram on page 246, cut one half into a cylinder shape and one half into a camera shape.

Lightly coat the camera pieces with buttercream. Roll 25 g/1 oz of the white sugarpaste out to a disc wide enough to cover the end of the lens and press into place. Roll out a quarter of the black sugarpaste to a strip wide enough to wrap round the lens. Smooth into place and mark on a square pattern with a knife. Roll out half the remaining black sugarpaste and cover the body of the camera, press into place, then stand on top of the cake and place the lens in front of it.

Roll the remaining black sugarpaste out into a long, thin strip about 30 cm/ 12 inches long and 5 cm/2 inches wide. Colour the remaining white sugarpaste pink and roll into two thin strips about 2 cm/³/₄ inch wide. Stick the strips on either side of the black strap with a little cold boiled water. Mark ridges onto the strap with a knife and drape the strap in position in front of the camera.

Carnival Cupcakes

Makes 12

For the cakes:

1 batch chocolate cupcakes
(*see* page 33)

To decorate:

1 batch cream cheese frosting
(*see* page 44)
pink and purple paste
food colourings
350 g/12 oz ready-to-roll
sugarpaste
icing sugar, for dusting
1 tbsp royal icing (*see* page 50)
or a small tube
small edible silver balls

Trim the tops of the cakes flat if they have peaked slightly. Colour the frosting deep pink and place in a large piping bag fitted with a star nozzle.

Colour half of the sugarpaste pink and half purple. Model the pink sugarpaste into six small carnival masks using a mould or by hand, then roll out the scraps thinly on a surface dusted with icing sugar and stamp out 18 tiny stars using a star cutter. Leave to dry out on nonstick baking parchment for 2 hours. Repeat with the purple sugarpaste. When firm enough to handle, stick the pink stars onto the purple masks and the purple stars onto the pink masks as shown, using a little royal icing to secure them.

Pipe the pink frosting onto the cakes in large swirls, then place the masks in the frosting as shown. Sprinkle over edible silver balls to finish.

Camping Fun Cake

Serves 20

For the cake:

1 x 23 cm/9 inch, square
chocolate cake
(*see* page 27)
1 x 13 cm/5 inch, square
chocolate cake

To decorate:

2 batches vanilla buttercream
green, orange, grey, red, blue,
brown and turquoise paste
food colourings
700 g/1½ lb ready-to-roll
sugarpaste
icing sugar, for dusting
chocolate drops
mini marshmallows

Colour half the buttercream pale green and smooth over the top and sides of the large cake with a palette knife. Place the cake on a cake board. Cut the smaller cake in half and stack one half on top of the other, sandwiching with buttercream. Cut away two sides to form a sloping roof for the tent.

Colour 450 g/1 lb sugarpaste orange, 75 g/3 oz grey, 50 g/2 oz red, 25 g/1 oz blue, 50 g/2 oz dark green and 25 g/1 oz brown. Roll out the orange sugarpaste on a surface dusted with icing sugar and use to cover the tent (*see* page 62), re-roll the scraps and cut out tent flaps and trims and stick in place with a little cold boiled water. Roll the orange scraps into short lengths for logs. Place a pile by the tent, then pile up more to make the fire. Make a ring of chocolate drops round the fire. Roll the grey sugarpaste into small balls and make two lines across the cake as shown. Colour half of the remaining buttercream light blue and spread between these grey pebbles to make a river, flicking up with a small palette knife. Press the dark green sugarpaste through a garlic press to make grass and arrange as shown. Model the red sugarpaste into a cube and top with white sugarpaste, then make a white lid for the cool bag. Roll the blue sugarpaste into a sausage and cut to make the cans. Place a white disc on each can and place in the cool bag. Mould the brown sugarpaste into a chimney and axe handle, position as shown and make a grey blade for the axe. Paint the logs with brown food colouring, add red scraps for flames, then attach two mini marshmallows to cocktail sticks and place on the fire. Colour the remaining buttercream turquoise and use a star border to pipe around the cake base.

Fashion Fiend Shoe Cake

Serves 20

For the cake base:

1 x 20 cm/8 inch, square Madeira
cake (*see* page 28)
1 bought trifle sponge square
1 bought mini Swiss roll

To decorate:

¹/₂ batch vanilla buttercream
1.3 kg/3 lb ready-to-roll sugarpaste
icing sugar, for dusting
pink and black paste food
colourings

Trim the top of the cake if it has peaked and cut the cake in half horizontally. Spread the buttercream over one half, then sandwich the layers back together. Spread the top and sides of the cake with buttercream. Roll out 700 g/1¹/₂ lb sugarpaste on a surface dusted with icing sugar and use to cover the cake (*see* page 62). Trim the edges neatly, then place on a cake board. Gather up the trimmings and colour half the remaining sugarpaste pink and half black.

Cut the trifle sponge into a triangular shape and spread with buttercream. Roll out the black sugarpaste thinly and cover the triangle neatly. Repeat with the mini Swiss roll, stand it upright, cut away a slope from the top and press the base out to represent a shoe heel. Roll a black sole shape from black sugarpaste and leave this to dry for 2 hours, draped over the side of a small upturned pudding basin lined with clingfilm, to make a curved shape. Roll out the remaining black sugarpaste and cut into random curved shapes and stick to the sides of the cake with a little cold boiled water. Roll the pink sugarpaste into 52 small pink balls and press round the base of the cake. Roll the remaining pink sugarpaste out thinly and cut out a curved shape for the centre of the cake as shown, dampen lightly and stick into place. Roll out the pink trimmings and decorate the triangular shoe front and the top of the curved sole shape. Decorate the pink shoe front with small black balls of sugarpaste and position the shoe front on the pink sugarpaste. Dampen the top of the heel section, stick the back of the sole to this and carefully position the other end of the sole behind the shoe front.

Stacked Suitcases Cake

Serves 20

For the cake:

To make these deep cakes, use
enough mixture to make
2 x 20 cm/8 inch Madeira cakes and
divide between 1 x 15 cm/6 inch
square tin and 1 x 20 cm/8 inch
square tin
(*see* page 28)

To decorate:

1 batch vanilla buttercream
1.5 kg/3 lb 3 oz ready-to-roll
sugarpaste
icing sugar, for dusting
ivory paste food colouring
gold lustre powder
edible icing pen (optional)

Trim the tops of the cakes flat if they have peaked and trim off one side of each cake to make them slightly oblong. Spread the buttercream over the top and sides of both cakes. Using 1.1 kg/2 lb 5 oz sugarpaste, cover the cakes following the instructions on page 62 and stack them up on a 25 cm/10 inch, round cake board. Press a ruler or the back of a knife a couple of times around the sides of each cake to mark where the suitcase would open.

Colour 250 g/9 oz sugarpaste ivory and, using three quarters of it, roll out long sausages to fit around the tops and bases of the cakes. Attach these with a little cold boiled water.

Roll out pieces of white and the leftover ivory sugarpaste on a surface dusted with icing sugar and cut out the lock, handle and strap details as shown and attach them with a little cold boiled water. A plastic drinking straw is a good tool to make the holes in the straps.

Roll out any leftover white sugarpaste very thinly and cut out luggage labels. Attach them with a little water and, when dry, paint details with a little gold lustre powder mixed with a little water – you can even write a name and address with an edible icing pen, if wished.

Catwalk Cupcakes

Makes 12

For the cakes:

1 batch chocolate cupcakes
(*see* page 33)

To decorate:

¹/₂ batch flower paste
(*see* page 48)
hot pink and black paste
food colourings
tiny edible silver seed pearls
1 batch vanilla buttercream

Divide the flower paste in half and colour one half hot pink and the rest black. Model six high-heeled shoes from the pink flower paste and six from the black, pressing tiny silver seed pearls into the sides of the shoes before the paste hardens. Leave the shoes on nonstick baking parchment for 2 hours to dry and become hard.

Trim the tops of the cupcakes if they have peaked. Reserve 2 tablespoons of the buttercream and colour this black. Colour the rest of the buttercream hot pink.

Spoon the pink buttercream into a large piping bag fitted with a star nozzle and pipe large swirls over the tops of the cupcakes, starting at the outside of each one and working towards the centre. Scatter tiny silver seed pearls over the top of each.

Stand a shoe on top of each cupcake, pressing it down gently into the buttercream. Using the frosting left in the bag, pipe a small rosette of pink buttercream on the front of each pink shoe. Spoon the black buttercream into a small piping bag fitted with a star nozzle and pipe rosettes on the front of the black shoes.

Sunshine Railway Cake

Serves 12–14

For the cake:

1 x 20 cm/8 inch, round chocolate
cake (*see* page 27)
1 mini chocolate Swiss roll
2 bought cake bars

To decorate:

1/2 batch vanilla buttercream
1.75 kg/31/2 lb ready-to-roll
sugarpaste
blue, green, orange, yellow, red,
turquoise, brown, grey and black
paste food colourings
icing sugar, for dusting
black bootlace liquorice strips
small candle
edible silver balls

Cut the cake in half, spread 1 half with buttercream and sandwich together. Spread the top and sides thinly with buttercream, using the remainder to coat the mini Swiss roll and cake bars. Colour 225 g/8 oz sugarpaste light blue, 350 g/12 oz light green, 125 g/4 oz dark green, 125 g/4 oz orange, 50 g/2 oz yellow, 50g/2 oz red, 125 g/4 oz turquoise, 125 g/4 oz brown, 125 g/4 oz grey, 25 g/1 oz black and leave the rest white. Cover the cake top with rolled light blue sugarpaste and the sides with light green. Place on a large board, half-covered with the remaining green sugarpaste as shown. Roll the brown sugarpaste into 6 cm/21/2 inch railway sleepers and the grey paste into two rail tracks and attach both as shown. Model the dark green sugarpaste into trees and white sugarpaste into trunks and stick onto the sides of the cake.

Cover the mini Swiss roll with turquoise sugarpaste. Cut cake bars to make 2 carriages, a funnel and cabin for the engine. Cover the funnel with black and blue sugarpastes and the cabin with blue sugarpaste. Cover the carriages with trimmings. Thickly roll the orange and yellow sugarpastes and cut a number 2 and a sunshine. Leave to dry on nonstick baking parchment until firm. Cut out carriage roofs and stick in place. Assemble the train pieces on the track. Make wheels from red sugarpaste. Cut the liquorice and stick to the wheels and carriage roofs. Decorate the carriages, engine and sunshine as shown. Make and decorate a small sugarpaste cake as shown. Roll white sugarpaste into clouds and a strip for a message. Stamp out white daisies with daisy stamps and attach with a silver ball in each. Paint the track and cake sides with green colouring. Attach the number 2 and sunshine to finish.

Off to See the World Cake

Serves 16

For the cake base:

1 x 20 cm/8 inch, round lemon
Madeira cake (*see* page 28)
6 tbsp apricot glaze

To decorate:

1.1 kg/2^1/$_2$ lb ready-to-roll
sugarpaste
dark blue and leaf green paste
food colourings
icing sugar, for dusting
candles

Trim the top of the cake if it has peaked, then brush the apricot glaze over the top and sides of the cake.

Colour 900 g/2 lb of the sugarpaste dark blue, then roll it out on a board dusted with icing sugar to a round large enough to cover the top and sides of the cake. Using both hands, carefully lift over the cake and smooth down. Trim the bottom edge neatly, then transfer the cake to a board or plate.

Colour the remaining sugarpaste leaf green and roll it out to about 5 mm/^{1}/$_4$ inch thick.

Trace the map of the world template on page 254 onto nonstick baking parchment and cut round the different continents with scissors. Place the cut-outs on the rolled-out green sugarpaste and cut around each piece. Dampen the undersides of the cut-outs by brushing with a little cold boiled water and press gently into position of the top of the cake. Add candles to finish.

Pretty Handbag Cake

Serves 12–16

For the cake base:

1 x 25 cm/10 inch, round
Madeira cake
(*see* page 28)

To decorate:

200 g/7 oz flower paste
(*see* page 48)
icing sugar, for dusting
brown and pink paste food colourings
1¹/₂ batches vanilla buttercream
700 g/1¹/₂ lb ready-to-roll sugarpaste
¹/₄ batch royal icing (*see* page 50)
gold lustre powder

Roll out the flower paste on a surface dusted with icing sugar and cut out two 2 x 23 cm/1 x 9 inch strips and four 2.5 x 5 cm/1 x 2 inch strips. Loop the shorter strips in half as shown and secure with a little cold boiled water. Add a tiny ball of white to each for the rivets. Do the same with the ends of the longer strips and then arrange them as shown, hanging over a bottle or rolling pin to dry. With the offcuts, model the tassel, then colour a little light brown to make the zip and tassel top.

Cut the cake in half across the middle and sandwich the halves together with half the buttercream. Stand the cake up on the cut edge and trim all round to make a smooth bag shape. Cover with the rest of the buttercream.

Colour 700 g/1¹/₂ lb sugarpaste pink then roll out to a piece large enough to cover the cake. Lift this carefully over the cake and smooth down the top and sides. Press an indentation where the zip will fit. Trim round the base and place on a large plate.

Roll out the remaining white sugarpaste into long sausages to fit all round the base of the cake and two strips over the top. Attach these and the rest of the decorations with dots of royal icing.

Make tiny sausages from the scraps of light brown flower paste and tuck them into the handles to look like links, then paint them with gold lustre powder mixed with a little water to finish.

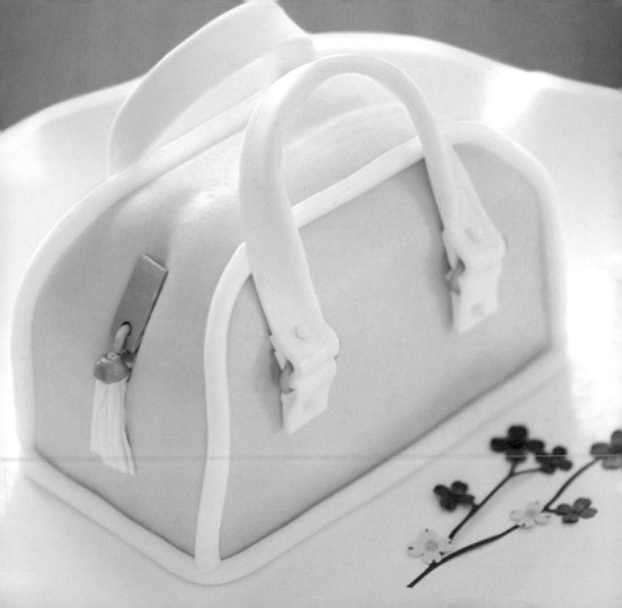

Rugby Ball Cupcakes

Makes 12

For the cakes:

1 batch chocolate cupcakes
(see page 33)

To decorate:

125 g/4 oz ready-to-roll
sugarpaste
brown and green paste
food colourings
1 batch vanilla buttercream

Colour 75 g/3 oz sugarpaste dark brown and leave the remainder white. Roll the brown sugarpaste into 12 small balls, then shape each ball into an oval. Roll the white sugarpaste into a thin sausage between your palms, then place thin strips onto the top of each rugby ball to represent the laces as shown.

Trim the tops of the cakes flat if they have peaked. Colour the buttercream bright green, then place the buttercream in a paper piping bag fitted with a no 2 straight nozzle. Press the nozzle of the piping bag onto the top of a cupcake and pipe out a small green dot. Pull the bag away to make a point then continue piping all over the top of each cake, carefully filling in all the spaces to represent grass.

Place a rugby ball in the centre of each cake to finish.

Disco Diva Cake

Serves 40

For the cake base:

1 x 20 cm/8 inch, round chocolate cake (*see* page 27)
1 x 15 cm/6 inch, round chocolate cake

To decorate:

1¹/₂ batches vanilla buttercream
1.8 kg/4 lb ready-to roll sugarpaste
pink and brown paste food colourings
icing sugar, for dusting
44 brown and 44 white chocolate-coated ball sweets (Maltesers)
floristry wires

Cut the tops of both cakes level if they have peaked, then cut each in half and spread one half with a little buttercream. Sandwich the cakes back together, then spread the remaining buttercream thinly over the top and sides. Colour 900 g/2 lb sugarpaste pink. Cover the larger cake with 700 g/1¹/₂ lb white sugarpaste (*see* page 62), and repeat with the smaller cake, using 450 g/1 lb pink sugarpaste to cover. Place the larger cake on a thin, 15 cm/6 inch cake board, then stack the small cake on top.

Reserve 125 g/4 oz pink sugarpaste. Colour half of the remaining pink sugarpaste a darker pink and the remaining 225 g/8 oz white sugarpaste brown. Roll out both pink sugarpastes thinly, cut into strips 2.5 cm/1 inch wide and stick to the sides of the larger cake with a little cold boiled water. Roll the reserved pink sugarpaste into a long strip 4 cm/1¹/₂ inches wide, dampen and press round the cake as shown. Press the sweets round the base of each cake as shown. Mould the trimmings into a bow (*see* page 63) and attach. Roll out the remainders and stamp out 15 small pink stars and 1 brown star with a cutter, and cut out the letters 'DIVA' in brown, using cutters or template on page 251. Thread wires into the stars and leave the stars and 'DIVA' letters to dry flat on nonstick baking parchment for 2 hours until firm.

Re-roll the trimmings and cut out large and small discs in pink, darker pink and brown, and stick to the sides of the cake with a little cold boiled water. Stand the letters on top of the cake, pushing some of the stars on wires in behind them for support. Position the remaining stars on wires as shown.

Baby Blue Car Cake

Serves 10–12

For the cake base:

20 cm/8 inch, round Madeira cake
(*see* page 28)
1 bought Madeira cake bar

To decorate:

³/₄ batch vanilla buttercream
1.3 kg/2 lb 14 oz ready-to-roll
sugarpaste
cream and blue paste
food colourings
icing sugar, for dusting
floristry wire (optional)

Trim the top of the cake flat if it has peaked and spread two thirds of the buttercream over the top and sides. Colour 650 g/1 lb 7 oz of the sugarpaste cream and use to cover the cake (*see* page 62). Trim, then place the cake on a 25 cm/10 inch cake board and cover the edges of the board with the trimmings.

Reserving 100 g/3¹/₂ oz for the details on the car, colour the rest of the sugarpaste bright blue. Roll out 175 g/6 oz of it on a surface dusted with icing sugar and, using the template on page 255, cut out 14 little cars. Mark the door detail on each and stick round the sides of the cake with a little cold boiled water. Press two tiny balls of white onto the wheels.

Carve the shape of the car body from the Madeira cake bar (chill the cake first, *see* page 60), then spread with the remaining buttercream. Roll out 200 g/7 oz blue sugarpaste and use it to smoothly cover the car cake. To raise the car off the 'ground', place it on a thick slab of 150 g/5 oz white sugarpaste, slightly smaller than the car base, on the top of the main cake. Roll out the remaining white sugarpaste and cut out windows, lights and a radiator and four wheels. Attach these with a little cold boiled water.

Roll the remaining blue sugarpaste into small balls and press round the base of the cake to finish. If liked, add a few balls of blue and white sugarpastes pushed onto curled floristry wire pressed into the cake. Remove these before serving.

Cricket Crazy Cake

Serves 10–12

For the cake base:

1 x 20 cm/8 inch, round
Madeira cake
(see page 28)

To decorate:

1.1 kg/2 lb 6 oz ready-to-roll
sugarpaste
black, brown, green, pink, red and
tan paste food colourings
icing sugar, for dusting
1 batch vanilla buttercream
small amount royal icing
(see page 50)
small tube writing icing
green ribbon trim

Colour 100 g/3½ oz sugarpaste black, roll out on a surface dusted with icing sugar and cut out enough 2 cm/¾ inch squares for your message. Leave to dry on nonstick baking parchment. Colour 75 g/3 oz sugarpaste brown and model the trophy as shown using bits of white to make the labels. Leave to dry on nonstick baking parchment until firm.

Trim the top of the cake flat if it has peaked and cover with buttercream. Colour 700 g/1½ lb sugarpaste green and use to cover the cake (see page 62). Trim, then place the cake on a 25 cm/10 inch cake board. Cover the edges of the board with the trimmings.

Using 175 g/6 oz white sugarpaste, make the cricketer – take half, roll into a sausage about 15 cm/6 inches long, flatten, trim, fold in half and hang over the side of the cake, attaching with a little cold boiled water. Use the rest to make the body, arms and feet and attach them with a little water. Colour 40 g/1½ oz sugarpaste pink and make the hands and head from small balls, pressing features into them with a knife or modelling tool. Attach the head with a cocktail stick. Colour the remaining sugarpaste red and tan to make a ball, bat, stumps and hair, attaching them all with a little cold boiled water. With black paste colouring mixed with a little water, paint the trophy label and features on the face. Paint a little pink colouring on his cheeks and nails. With royal icing and a small writing tube, pipe markings on the cricket ball and letters on the black tiles. Stick these and the trophy onto the cake with dots of royal icing. Trim with a green ribbon around the board.

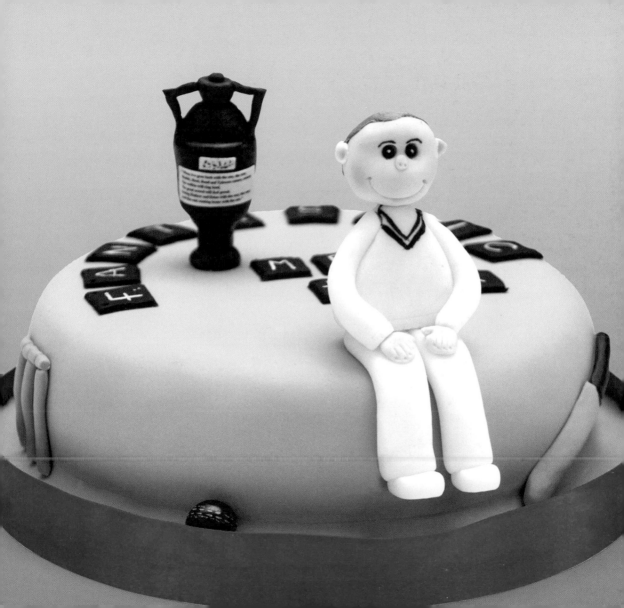

Truck Driver Cake

Serves 8–12

For the cake base:

1 bought mini cake bar
20 cm/8 inch, square Madeira cake
(*see* page 28)
8 tbsp apricot glaze

To decorate:

1.3 kg/2 lb 13 oz ready-to-roll
sugarpaste
red, black, orange and green paste
food colourings
icing sugar, for dusting
silver lustre powder
small amount royal icing
(*see* page 50)
50 g/2 oz fudge chunks

Chill the cake bar in the freezer. Colour 25 g/1 oz sugarpaste red, then roll out thickly on a surface dusted with icing sugar and cut out two road signs. Press a damp cocktail stick into the side. Repeat with 25 g/1 oz white sugarpaste. Leave to dry.

Trim the top of the cake flat if it has peaked, then brush most of the apricot glaze over the cake. Cover the cake with 750 g/1 lb 10 oz white sugarpaste (*see* page 62). Trim and place on a 22 cm/9 inch plate or board.

Colour 200 g/7 oz sugarpaste black, 200 g/7 oz orange and 150 g/5 oz pale green. For the road, roll out 100 g/3$^{1}/_{2}$ oz black, cut out a strip to fit across the cake and attach with a little cold boiled water. Use 25 g/1 oz of the orange sugarpaste to model two traffic cones with a small strip of white sugarpaste around each. For the truck, brush the mini cake bar with the remaining apricot glaze, roll out half the remaining orange sugarpaste and cover. Model the orange cab as shown, adding black details. Stand the truck on a small block of black sugarpaste on the cake and stick on wheels made from flattened paste balls, brushing the centres with silver lustre powder mixed with a little water.

Using royal icing, pipe details on the signs, a line down the centre and sides of the road plus dots on top of the lorry. Press on chopped fudge chunks. Roll out the green sugarpaste and cut circles using a fluted pastry cutter, cut in half and stick round the base. Press on the road signs and cones to finish.

Jolly Clown Cake

Serves 20–24

For the cake base:

1 x 25 cm/10 inch all-in-one quick-mix sponge made in 1 x 20 cm/8 inch, round tin and 1 x 20 cm/8 inch, square tin (*see* page 30)

To decorate:

225 g/8 oz desiccated coconut
orange liquid food colouring
3 batches vanilla buttercream
various coloured sweets and jellies

Put 50 g/2 oz coconut in a bowl and, while stirring, add drops of orange food colouring until the coconut is sufficiently coloured.

Cover the round cake with one third of the buttercream and position it towards the bottom of a large board.

Following the template on page 245, cut up the square cake and cover each piece with most of the remaining buttercream.

Scatter the white coconut on a sheet of nonstick baking parchment and dip the pieces into it, assembling them on the board as shown. Repeat with the orange coconut and the hairpieces, then position them and scatter orange coconut across the top of the head to join up the hair. Use up any leftover buttercream and coconut to tidy up any holes.

Press sweets and jellies onto the cake to make the face and decorate the bow tie and hat.

Heels Flowers Cupcakes

Makes 12

For the cakes:

1 batch vanilla cupcakes
(*see* page 33)
2 tbsp apricot glaze

To decorate:

875 g/1³/₄ lb ready-to-roll sugarpaste
pink, green, yellow and purple paste
food colourings
icing sugar, for dusting
edible pearls and tiny coloured balls

Colour 225 g/8 oz of the sugarpaste pink, 225 g/8 oz lime green, 225 g/8 oz yellow and 125 g/4 oz purple.

Trim the cupcakes to give them a rounded shape and brush the apricot glaze over. Roll out the pink sugarpaste thinly on a board or surface dusted with icing sugar. Using a round cutter, stamp out four circles 6 cm/2¹/₂ inches wide. Repeat with the green and yellow sugarpastes, and re-roll the scraps.

Dust the inside of an embossing pattern mould lightly with icing sugar and flick away the excess with a soft paintbrush. Press the circle of pink sugarpaste into the mould, pressing around the pattern, then lift it out carefully and drape the paste over the cupcake. Press the sugarpaste into position, being careful not to touch the design.

Press the plain green and yellow discs onto the remaining 8 cakes. Using an embossing mould and daisy stamps, cut out yellow and pink petals and decorate the pink cakes. Stick the pieces in place with a little cold boiled water. Using shoe moulds, green strips and small pink stars decorate the yellow cakes. Stamp out pink daisies, purple daisy centres and an embossed pink flower to decorate the green cakes. Stamp out tiny purple stars and press them onto the cakes. To finish, press coloured and pearl balls into the centres of the daisies.

Flying Pilot Cake

Serves 12–14

For the cake base:

1 x 20 cm/8 inch, round lemon
Madeira cake (*see* page 28)

To decorate:

$^1/_4$ batch lemon buttercream
1.5 kg/3$^1/_3$ lb ready-to-roll
sugarpaste
blue, red, orange, black, brown
and flesh toned paste
food colourings
icing sugar, for dusting
6 medium and 10 mini
marshmallows
1 mini Swiss roll
blue trim

Trim the top of the cake flat if it has peaked and spread the buttercream over the top and sides. Colour 700 g/1$^1/_2$ lb sugarpaste blue. Use to cover the cake as per the instructions on page 62. Trim, then place the cake on a 25 cm/10 inch cake board and cover the edges of the board with blue trimmings.

Roll out 275 g/10 oz white sugarpaste thinly. Cut out cloud shapes, dampen lightly with cold boiled water and press onto the top and sides. Roll out thin scraps and wrap around 10 small and 6 medium-size marshmallows, for the fluffy clouds, smoothing over the joins. Place on top of the cake.

Colour 225 g/8 oz of the sugarpaste red, 25 g/1 oz orange, 15 g/$^1/_2$ oz black, 15 g/$^1/_2$ oz brown and 50 g/2 oz for the skin. Roll out a little red paste, cut out the wings and fins of the plane and leave to dry on nonstick baking parchment for 2 hours. Make a small hollow in a mini Swiss roll, then roll out the remaining red paste to an oval large enough to cover it. Smooth over, keeping the joins underneath, and place in the middle of the clouds. Model the pilot's head, body and arms with the skin-coloured sugarpaste and place the body in the cockpit. Roll out some orange sugarpaste thinly and make the jacket, propeller and wing trims. Stick on the jacket, make brown hair for the head and mark on the face. Secure the head onto the body with a cocktail stick. Roll, cut out and attach the finishing details, rest the wings on the clouds and attach the fins at the back. Add the blue trim to finish.

Cake Cutting Guides & Templates

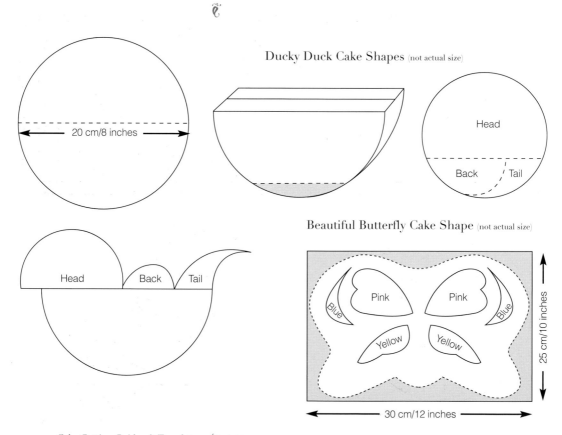

20 cm/8 inches

Ducky Duck Cake Shapes (not actual size)

Head

Back   Tail

Head   Back   Tail

Beautiful Butterfly Cake Shape (not actual size)

Blue   Pink   Pink   Blue

Yellow   Yellow

25 cm/10 inches

30 cm/12 inches

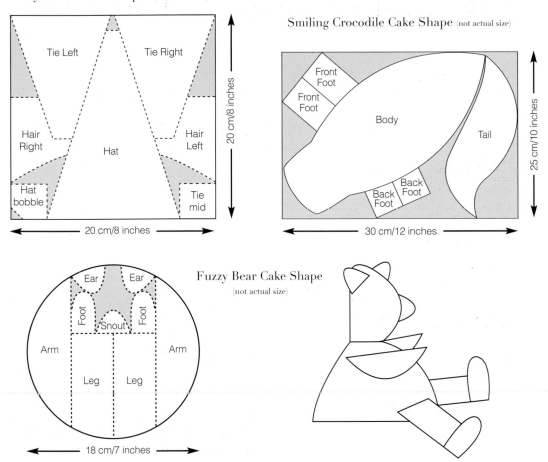

Jolly Clown Cake Shapes (not actual size)

Tie Left
Tie Right

Hair Right
Hair Left

Hat

Hat bobble
Tie mid

20 cm/8 inches
20 cm/8 inches

Smiling Crocodile Cake Shape (not actual size)

Front Foot
Front Foot

Body

Tail

Back Foot
Back Foot

25 cm/10 inches
30 cm/12 inches

Fuzzy Bear Cake Shape
(not actual size)

Ear
Ear

Foot
Snout
Foot

Arm
Arm

Leg
Leg

18 cm/7 inches

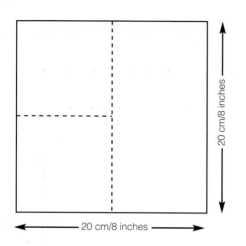

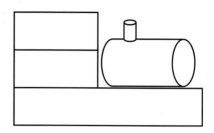

20 cm/8 inches

20 cm/8 inches

My Camera Cake Shapes (not actual size)

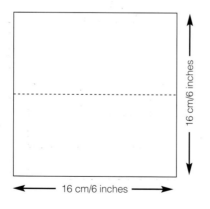

16 cm/6 inches

16 cm/6 inches

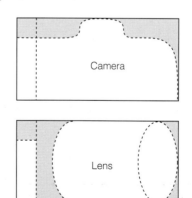

Camera

Lens

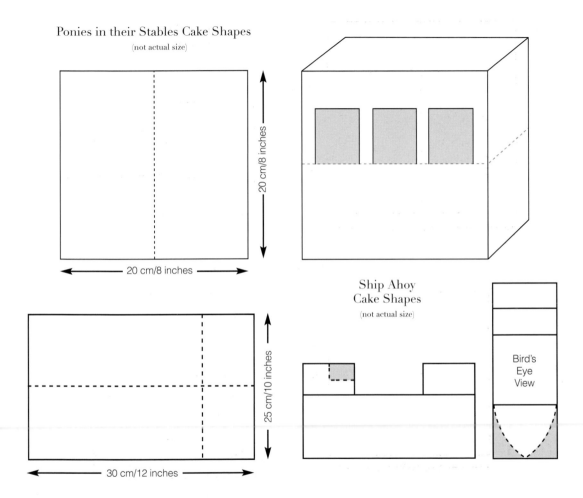

Ponies in their Stables Cake Shapes
(not actual size)

20 cm/8 inches

20 cm/8 inches

Ship Ahoy
Cake Shapes
(not actual size)

25 cm/10 inches

30 cm/12 inches

Bird's
Eye
View

Farmyard Friends Cow Template

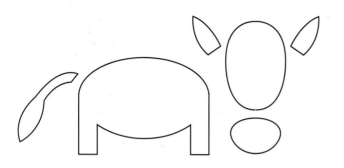

Finished Cow

Farmyard Friends Horse Template

Finished Horse

Farmyard Friends Pig Template

Finished Pig

Farmyard Friends Sheep Template

Finished Sheep

Farmyard Friends Chicken Template

Finished Chicken

Here are suggested shapes to cut out for your farmyard friends, along with how to arrange them into the finished designs.

Genie Lamp Template

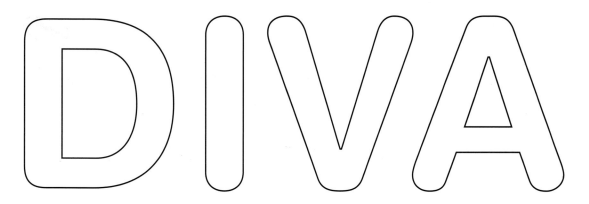

Disco Diva Cake Letters
Templates

Magic Garden Cake Butterfly Template

Beautiful Butterfly
Cupcake Template

Starbright Fireworks Cupcakes Star Template

Lovestruck Tiered Cake Hearts Templates

Under the Sea Cake Starfish Template

Buzzy Bee Cupcakes Flower Template

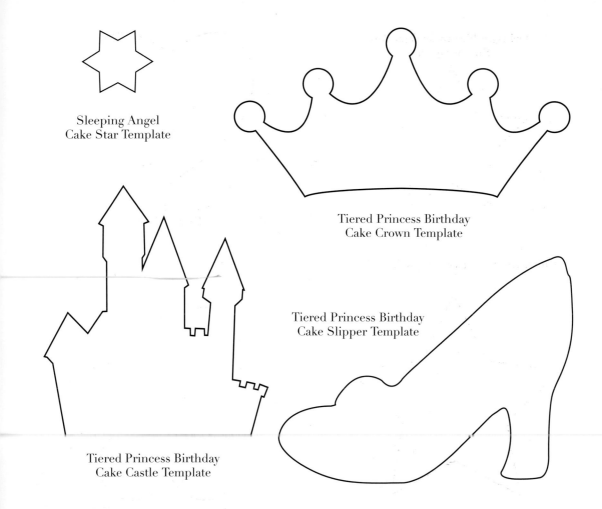

Sleeping Angel
Cake Star Template

Tiered Princess Birthday
Cake Crown Template

Tiered Princess Birthday
Cake Slipper Template

Tiered Princess Birthday
Cake Castle Template

Off To See The World Template

Baby Blue Car Cake Template

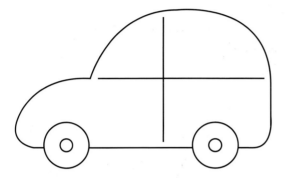

Patchwork Bears Christening Cake Template

Teddies in Tutus Cupcakes Template/Guide

Carnival Cupcakes Mask and Star Templates/Guides

Index